The Coldest Day of the Year

The Coldest Day of the Year

True (Fall and Winter) Stories from a Wisconsin Farm

(Book Number 5 in the Series)

LeAnn R. Ralph

Dedication

Anyone who has lived on a farm knows that animals, large and small, are an integral part of daily life, even the dogs and cats. The year 2008 was a bad one for losing many of my animal companions. They were more than friends. They were members of my family. Guinevere, Winifred and Duke were part of the litter of kittens I rescued when they were two weeks old after their momma was killed defending her babies from a Doberman-German Shepherd cross. Their brother, Tiger Paw Thompson, died in 2004. Simon Peter was a very sick barn kitten. In spite of different antibiotics and subcutaneous fluids, he didn't make it. Of all the barn kittens in recent years, he was the only long-haired kitten. Charlie was our Springer Spaniel and my constant companion for "all things outside." One day I will find each of you at the Rainbow Bridge.

In loving memory...

Guinevere (May 15, 1991 to January 1, 2008)
Winifred (May 15, 1991 to May 21, 2008)
Duke (May 15, 1991 to June 22, 2008)
Simon Peter (May 1, 2008 to June 25, 2008)
Charlie (May 30, 1995 to July 11, 2008)

~ Foreword ~

My mission of documenting farm life on a small family dairy farm in West Central Wisconsin 40 years ago continues in *The Coldest Day of the Year*, the fifth book in the Rural Route 2 series. When I was a kid, if someone had told me that virtually all of the small farms with 20 or 30 cows (where the cows had names!) would one day be gone, I would not have believed it.

LeAnn R. Ralph
Colfax, Wisconsin

~ 1 ~
Indian Summer

The October sunshine felt warm on my face as I set my book on the ground. The teacher had assigned a book report, and I had been reading the book on the one-hour bus ride to and from school. We only lived six miles from town, but I was the first one on the bus and the last one off. The book was about a girl who loved horses. Her big sister was a professional horse trainer, and she wanted to be a horse trainer, too.

While the bus began to back out of the driveway, I tied my light-blue button-down sweater around my waist. Whenever I tied a sweater around my waist, I felt like I was wearing an apron backwards.

My mother never wore an apron when she worked in the kitchen at home, but she and the other ladies wore aprons when they worked in the kitchen at church. The aprons were lacy, frilly things. One lady wore a sheer white one, like the curtains in our kitchen, with white lace around the edge and yellow daffodils on the pockets. I never could figure out how those aprons would protect a dress. Mom said when all you were doing was pouring coffee and serving cookies, there wasn't much to spill.

I leaned down to pick up my books. A few feet away, the spring gurgled quietly as it trickled down the hill next to the driveway. In the little pasture on the other side of the driveway, the dairy cows stood in groups of two or three, although some of them were lying down, legs tucked under them.

The cows had eaten all of the grass next to the fence posts and underneath the strands of barbed wire, but beyond where they could reach, the grass next to the driveway was long. The grass had been white with frost when I walked down the hill this morning to get on the bus, but this afternoon the frost was gone and the grass was green again.

During the summer, Dad clipped the edge of the driveway once with the hay mower, and after that, it was left to grow up again. My big sister, Loretta, said it was too bumpy to mow along the driveway with the push mower. Loretta was nineteen years older than me, and my big brother, Ingman, was twenty-one years older. Mom had been stricken with polio when she was twenty-six years old. After that, the doctors told her she would never have more children. I was born sixteen years later.

"Mooooooo," said one of the cows standing close to the fence.

"Moooo-ooooo-oooo," said another one next to her.

It was Rags and Patches, the first twin heifers I had ever seen on our farm. They were Holsteins. When Rags and Patches were babies, I had spent almost every evening while I was in the barn to help Dad with the milking combing the long curls at the end of their tails. Some cows had a bushy tail at the bottom and some had curlicues. Rags and Patches had curlicues. Most of our cows were Holsteins, although we had few Guernseys in the herd, too, and one little Jersey.

"Hi, Rags! Hi, Patches!" I said.

"Moo!" said Patches.

Rags did not say anything at all except to toss her head and waggle her ears.

I started up the driveway, and when I was almost as far as the maple tree in the front lawn, I cut across the ditch and headed up the steep bank. I had taken this route so many times I had worn a path in the long grass. The lawn was much too steep here for the mower, and Dad couldn't get at it with the tractor. Tall stalks of Goldenrod with white feathery tatters that had once been yellow flowers waved gently in the breeze. In the warm afternoon sunshine, the silver maple leaves that littered the ground smelled sweet and reminded me of vanilla.

"Hi Dusty!" I said.

I could see my brown pony with the white mane and tail standing by the fence in her pasture at the edge of the lawn. The pony bobbed her head up and down. *"Her-her-her-her,"* she nickered.

I pushed aside some of the dry maple leaves to pick a small handful of grass. The lawn had not been cut in more than a month, but it was not growing very much anymore. Dad said it was better to leave it a little longer over winter because then it would come back better in the spring.

"Her-her-her-her," Dusty said again as I walked to the fence. I held my hand out flat. The pony's lips barely touched my palm, and

then the grass was gone. She made quick work of the small mouthful and pushed her nose toward my hand again, brown eyes gleaming from beneath the thick white foretop

"That's all I've got," I said. I held up my hand. "See?"

I reached forward to rub the pony's ears. Dusty twisted her head to one side. When she was satisfied that all of the itchiness was gone she turned her head so I could get at the other ear.

"I'd better go inside and change out of my school clothes now," I said.

As if the pony understood, she stepped back and began nosing around in the dry maple leaves at her feet.

I turned toward the house. Although it felt as warm as a summer day, I knew it was not summer. On a warm summer day, I would have heard red-winged blackbirds from the marsh below Dusty's pasture and orioles and robins and meadowlarks and barn swallows and bluebirds. But the birds had all gone south. And once the birds left, I knew winter was not very far away.

I switched my books to the other arm and headed across the lawn. Dad said that in another month, or maybe six weeks, we might have snow on the ground. I liked snow because then I could slide on the hill in the pasture next to the driveway where the cows were today. But I did not much care for winter when the temperature dropped below zero. Sometimes my feet got so cold in my thin black rubber chore boots that I would take off my boot and my shoe while I waited for more milk to carry to the milkhouse and would stand with my foot on a cow who had settled down for a nap.

Mom did not believe me when I told her that my feet got so cold I could not feel them and said I was only trying to get out of helping with the chores.

Dad said Mom did not believe me because it had been so many years since she was able to work outside in the winter that she could not remember what it was like.

The polio had left my mother partially paralyzed in one leg and completely paralyzed in the other. In the house, she got around by using her crutches and leaning on furniture. Outside, she always used her crutches. But Mom did not go outside very much in the winter, only from the house to the car. And if Dad was going to take her someplace, he would start the car ahead of time and let it run for a while to give the heater a chance to warm up before she got there.

I continued across the yard behind the house and walked past the lilacs. All the other trees had lost their leaves, but the lilac leaves were still green. Not bright green like they were in the spring, but still green. The lilacs, I knew, would not lose their leaves until the weather turned much colder and it was almost ready to snow.

As I walked past the last of the three lilacs that my grandmother had planted long before I was born, I could see our Cocker Spaniel-Spitz mix dog, Needles, lying in front of the machine shed door, nose on his paws. If Needles was staring into the machine shed, Dad must be inside. And sure enough, before I reached the porch steps, I could hear my father singing to himself—*lye-dee-dye-dee-doe; lye-dee-dye,dee-dee; lye-dee-dye-dee-dooooooooooe.*

The "lye-dee-doe" song did not mean anything at all. It was just something Dad sang to himself when he was in a good mood.

Needles lifted his head and turned to look at me. His feathery cream-colored tail thumped against the ground a couple of times, and then he went back to staring into the machine shed with his nose on his paws.

Wherever Dad was, Needles was sure to be close by, just in case my father started the tractor or decided to go somewhere in the pickup truck. Needles loved to ride in the truck or on the tractor with Dad. If Needles rode on the tractor, then my father would stand up to drive so the dog could sit on the seat.

I set my books on the porch steps and headed toward the machine shed.

"What're you doing, Daddy?" I asked.

"Trying to get the bucket on the tractor," my father replied.

The 460 Farmall was parked inside the machine shed, pulled up to the spot where Dad had taken the bucket off last spring. During the winter, Dad used the bucket to push snow out of the driveway and to leave it in big piles at the edge of the lawn.

"I thought you said it wasn't going to snow for a while yet," I said.

"It's not. Not that I know of. But I want to get the bucket on the tractor now so I can put the combine away. If I put the combine away before I get the bucket out of here, I won't be able to get *to* the bucket when I need it," he said.

"Oh," I said.

"I don't mind about the corn picker," Dad continued. "I can leave that outside over winter. But I don't want to leave the combine outside."

The only tractor we had that could pull the big red combine was the four-sixty. Dad used the combine to harvest oats in August, and then later on in the fall, he used it to harvest soybeans. For now, Dad had parked the combine in the pole shed, although soon, he would move it to the machine shed.

My father liked to park the tractor and the manure spreader in the pole shed during the winter because he could drive in one door and out the other. He kept the manure spreader in the shed so it would not fill up with snow. Cleaning the barn in the winter was enough work already, Dad said, without shoveling snow out of the manure spreader.

"You'd better go in the house and change your clothes," Dad said as he went back to the workbench. "Ma will be wondering what happened to you."

"Okay, Daddy," I said.

I bent down to pet the top of Needles' head. He rolled his round brown eyes in my direction while his tail swept back and forth along the ground. Now I knew why Needles was staring into the machine shed. Dad *was* doing something with the tractor.

A few minutes later I walked into the kitchen of our little white farmhouse.

"What did you learn in school today?" asked my mother. She was sitting by the table, peeling potatoes for supper. My mother could not stand up very well, so she always sat down to peel potatoes. Dad grew potatoes and other vegetables in our garden, and we often ate meat and mashed potatoes and homegrown vegetables for supper.

I set my books on the table and untied the light blue sweater from around my waist.

Every day when I came home from school, Mom asked what I had learned. Most of the time, it seemed like we had not really learned much of anything.

Today, though, I had something to tell her.

"We learned about Indian Summer," I said.

My mother stopped peeling and looked over at me. "It's not Indian Summer today."

"It's not?" I looked out the kitchen window where the sun was shining brightly, even though it had already started to drop lower in the sky. By the time we finished eating supper, it would be dark outside.

Mom shook her head and reached up to push back a lock of her curly brown hair that was so dark it was almost black. "No, it's not Indian Summer today," she said.

"But—our teacher said so."

"That's what the weatherman said on television this morning, too. But it's not Indian Summer," she replied.

The television sat in the corner of the living room on four sturdy legs and reminded me, for some reason, of the big green frogs that sunned themselves on the lily pads in the Norton Slough. We never saw the frogs in the evening if Dad and I went fishing after the milking was done. But if we went fishing on a warm, sunny, Sunday afternoon, the frogs would be crouched on their lily pads, and as we walked along the slough bank, they would jump off into the water with a splash.

"But why isn't it Indian Summer?" I asked. "Our teacher said it's Indian Summer when we get a warm, sunny day after it freezes."

My mother shrugged and began to cut the potato. *Ker-plunk, ker-plunk, ker-plunk* went the potato pieces as they dropped into the pan.

"Seemed like just another nice fall day to me," she said.

"Then what makes it Indian Summer?" I asked.

Mom reached for another potato. Often it was my job to fetch potatoes from the basement for supper. Sometimes, though, Mom asked Dad to go and get them when he came in the house for a cup of coffee during the afternoon.

"We have to get snow first before it's Indian Summer," she explained.

I looked out the window again at the clear blue sky.

"Snow? Does it have to snow a lot?" I asked, turning back toward Mom.

"No. Just a little bit. Then after it melts, and if we get some nice, warm, sunny days, then that's Indian Summer," she said.

"How come?"

My mother sighed. "Well, I don't know why, exactly. Except if it's a warm fall day, and we don't have snow, how is that any different than any other warm fall day?"

"I don't know," I said.

"But if we think it's going to be winter, like when it snows," she continued, "and then it turns warm and sunny again, then we think it's more like summer."

Maybe Mom was right, but still, if my teacher and the weatherman said it was Indian Summer...

"Did you just make that up?" I asked. "About it not being Indian Summer until after it snows?"

"No," my mother said, "I did not just make it up. That's what my mother and father always said."

My mother's folks, Nels and Inga, were immigrants from Norway who had both died long before I was born. Mom had a wedding picture of them. And I had seen a couple of other pictures of Inga, too, enough to know that my big sister, Loretta, looked like her.

"Does Norway have Indian Summer?" I asked.

My mother shook her head.

"Why not?"

"No Indians," she replied.

We had learned in school that American Indians were the first people who had lived here. But I didn't know if they had lived anywhere else before that.

"Aren't there any Indians in Norway?" I asked.

Mom shook her head. "Nope. No Indians in Norway. Used to be Indians around here, though."

"Really?"

My mother nodded and reached for another potato.

"Did Grandma Inga and Grandpa Nels know any Indians?" I asked.

After all, Caddie Woodlawn knew Indians, and she had lived in this part of Wisconsin a long time ago, too. We had been reading Caddie Woodlawn's books in school.

"No," Mom said, "my folks didn't know any Indians, although there were still a few around when my grandpa first came to live here. Or so I've heard."

"Did they call it Indian Summer?" I asked.

"Who?" Mom inquired.

"The Indians," I said.

My mother shook her head as she finished peeling the last potato. "I wouldn't have the foggiest notion if the Indians actually called it Indian Summer or not," she replied.

Mom put her hands on the chair seat, one on each side, and pushed herself up. She grabbed the table with one hand to steady herself.

"Go upstairs and change out of your school clothes. Then you can eat a snack. And then you can go and get the cows for Dad."

"Okay," I said. "But I don't have to go far for the cows. They're in the pasture right next to the driveway."

I changed my clothes and ate a slice of homemade bread with butter and blackberry jam. Mom had made the jam last summer after Dad and I had gone picking blackberries around the bottom of the big wooded hill behind the barn that we called The Bluff.

When I went outside a short while later, the cows were still in the little pasture next to the driveway. Dad stood in the barnyard and yelled "come boss," and they all hurried toward the barn so fast they were almost trotting.

After the cows were in the barn and the last stanchion was closed, I decided to ask Dad about Indian Summer.

"Was it Indian Summer today?" I said as I watched my father put the milker inflations together in the milkhouse.

Every day when Dad washed the milkers, he took them apart. The black rubber tubes had to be put back into the metal sleeves. Each milker had four inflations and sometimes he had to work hard to pull the top of the inflation through the metal tube. When the inflation finally pulled through, it made *snap-pop* sound.

Dad shrugged as he fitted one narrow end of an inflation onto the metal part that held them all together. "Ma says it has to snow first before it's Indian Summer."

"I know," I said. "That's what she told me too."

Dad reached for the next set of inflations.

"When do you think it might snow? So I can see what Indian Summer looks like?" I asked.

"Hard to tell," Dad said. "In the fall, the weather can turn from summer to winter overnight. But sometimes it stays cold and then we don't get any Indian Summer at all."

A few weeks later when I woke up in the morning, I was surprised to see that the ground was covered with a thin layer of white. The weather had not been especially cold the day before, and it was not enough snow to slide in the pasture with my toboggan. But it was still snow.

And because there was snow on the ground, Mom said I had to wear my winter coat. As I walked down the hill toward the bus, I pulled my hood up. For the first time since last winter, my ears felt cold, and I was glad that I had a hood.

By the time we went outside for morning recess most of the snow had melted, and by afternoon, it was so warm that I carried my coat when I walked up the hill from the bus.

And right then and there, I could see what Mom meant about how if it snows, we think it's going to be winter, but then if the weather turns warm again, it seems more like summer.

I still did not know why it was called Indian Summer, though.

~ 2 ~
Like Magic

Outside, it was a cold, dreary afternoon, and as I turned to the next page in my book, a fire crackled and sizzled and popped in the wood stove not far from my mother's chair. Mom spent many hours every day in her chair by the living room picture window. Sometimes she read the newspaper. Sometimes she worked on embroidering pillowcases and dresser scarves. Sometimes she just sat looking out the window to watch the cows in the pasture across the road from the driveway.

Today, though, she was paging through a catalog and looking—I hoped—for Christmas presents.

After I thought about it for a little while, I decided she probably was not looking for Christmas presents. Mom never did any Christmas shopping until after Thanksgiving. In Sunday school this morning, we had started practicing for the Sunday school Christmas program. And that meant Christmas was not very far away, even though it was still more than a month until Thanksgiving.

That's what our Sunday school teacher said, anyway—that it wasn't long until Christmas. As far as I was concerned, the Christmas program was not nearly far enough away. This morning the superintendent had handed out the parts we were supposed memorize. Mine was almost a half a page, and I was certain I would never be able to learn all of it.

I put my finger between the pages of the book to keep my place and reached over to pull the blanket tighter around my legs. I was curled up on the davenport across the living room from my mother. The book was one of my favorites. It was about a girl named Katie John. The girl was always getting into trouble. She didn't mean to get in trouble. She didn't start out to get into trouble. She didn't do things on purpose to get into trouble. But it seemed as if some things never quite turned out the way Katie John had planned.

I knew what that was like. One time when my big sister was sewing a new red velveteen dress for me for Christmas, I had kept on asking her questions. After a while, Loretta ended up sewing the dress to her finger. Mom said it was because I was talking too much.

When the blanket was tucked around my legs, instead of going back to reading, I sat and watched the big silver maple tree in the front lawn just outside the picture window. The gray branches were bare, and they bobbed back and forth and up and down in the east wind.

I knew the wind was blowing out of the east because every now and then, the living room window where Mom kept her African violets would rattle. My mother said she did not know why her African violets liked light from the east window, but anyone could see that they did. The plants were a deep, dark green, and they were covered with purple, pink and white flowers. Some had smooth petals and some were ruffled.

The east wind had already been blowing this morning while we were doing the chores. Dad said that with the wind out of the east like it was, it might snow tonight or tomorrow.

After we had finished the dinner dishes, I had gone outside to see Dusty. Even though I was wearing mittens, in just a few minutes, my hands turned numb. Dusty had been standing with her tail to the wind and with her head inside the old chicken coop Dad said she could use for a barn. Mom said she hoped that when it started snowing, Dusty would go inside the chicken coop, but I was pretty sure she would not. Dad and I had tried leading her into the chicken coop several times. Dusty willingly came inside with us, but as soon as we let go of her halter, she would turn around and go right back outside.

Needles had come out to Dusty's pasture with me. But when he saw I was not going to be doing anything very interesting, such as going for a walk around the cow paths at the bottom of the big wooded hill behind the barn, or taking Dusty out for a ride so he could follow along, he had gone back to the machine shed. Dad had left a folded up canvass tarp on the floor, and Needles had curled up on it with his nose buried in his fluffy cream-colored tail.

Feeling guilty, I had hurried back to the house to get out of the cold wind. Dusty was standing with her head in the chicken coop. Needles was curled up on a tarp in the machine shed. And I was going into the house where I knew my mother would put more wood into the woodstove to keep the living room warm...

I heaved a deep sigh, put my book down and sat up on the davenport.

My mother took off her reading glasses and looked over at me.

"It's so cold and dreary outside today, isn't it," she said. "I always think it's depressing at this time of year. The leaves are gone from the trees. The grass has stopped growing. And everything is just brown and gray without any snow to cover it."

She sat looking out the window for a moment before turning toward me. "I know just what we need to cheer us up," she said. "Let's bake a cake. What kind would you like? White, yellow, chocolate, pineapple-up-side-down or marble?"

I didn't even have to think about it.

"Marble!" I exclaimed.

"Good. That's what I was thinking, too. It's been quite awhile since I made a marble cake."

Actually, I could not remember the last time my mother had baked a marble cake.

To me it seemed like some sort of magic, this process of mixing together different ingredients that, separately, weren't anything at all like a cake. It was a little like mixing up milk replacer for the calves. The powdered milk replacer looked like white flour when it was still in the big brown paper bag that was almost waist high on me. But after I put water in the calf buckets, dumped in the dry milk replacer, and mixed it up with a paddle Dad had made out of an old board, it turned to light yellow, like the color of cake batter for a yellow cake after Mom had beaten in a couple of eggs.

My mother pushed herself up from the chair by the living room window and fitted her arms into the metal cuffs of her crutches. She swung one leg out from the hip, moved a crutch forward and swung the other leg out from the hip. I waited until she had made her way through the doorway and followed her into the kitchen.

Mom carefully set her crutches against the table and grabbed the back of one of the kitchen chairs to steady herself. She slowly turned and stretched out her arm. With her fingers inches from the sink, she let go of the chair, leaned forward and steadied herself on the edge of the counter.

"If you're going to help me bake a cake, you have to wash your hands, too," she said.

Standing side by side at the kitchen sink, we took turns washing our hands with a bar of Ivory soap. When we had dried our hands, Mom reached into the cupboard for a mixing bowl. "First we need butter, shortening and sugar," she said.

A stick of wrapped butter sat on the counter. Butter straight out of the refrigerator is too hard to use for baking so my mother must have already been thinking about making a cake even before she mentioned it in the living room. She had probably taken the butter out of the refrigerator right after we had finished washing the dinner dishes.

"Would you like to unwrap that?" Mom asked.

I slowly unwrapped the waxy paper and let the stick drop into the mixing bowl where it landed with a soft *plop*. Removing butter from the wrapper—especially soft butter—was one of those little tasks Mom found difficult because it required two hands, one to hold the stick and one to unfold the paper.

"Now I need some sugar," my mother said, pulling a copper canister toward her. My sister had given Mom the set of copper canisters for Christmas one year. The canisters looked like stair steps because each one was a step smaller than the one before it. The canister marked "flour" was the largest. The little canister on the end was marked "tea."

Mom measured out the sugar and shortening.

"Would you find the spatula for me, please?" she asked.

I opened another drawer and peered inside until I spotted the utensil. My big sister called it a rubber scraper, but Mom called it a spatula. Usually Loretta would bake something on a Sunday afternoon, but today she had gone upstairs right after dinner to lie down because she had a bad headache. Dad said Loretta might have a headache because it was going to snow. I asked why snow would give someone a headache. He said it was like when bad weather made a person's rheumatism act up. When I had asked what rheumatism was, Mom had said it was something old people got that made their joints ache.

I pulled out the spatula and held it toward my mother.

She laid it by the bowl. "Thank you. Now we have to stir this. Would you plug the mixer in for me, please?"

I carefully pushed the plug into the wall socket. The mixer whirred for a minute until my mother shut it off and propped it against the bowl.

"Next I need some eggs," she announced. "Will you get them from the refrigerator? And the milk, too?"

I brought out a carton of eggs and the pitcher of milk. Soon three eggs were mixed in with the other ingredients.

"Now we need to add milk, vanilla, salt, and baking powder. And after that comes the flour."

In no time at all, she had dumped in the next ingredients. Then she pulled open the flour bin, a large drawer next to the stove that could hold fifty pounds. Mom bought fifty pounds of flour and used the white flour sack material to make dishtowels.

I counted as my mother dipped into the bin. One...two...three cups went into the bowl.

"You're supposed to alternate the liquid and the flour," she explained as she reached down to push the drawer shut, "but that's kind of hard for me to do. So I just dump it all in at once. Haven't noticed it makes much difference to the cake."

I waited until Mom shut off the mixer again.

"Are you going to make the marble now?" I asked.

The "marble" was the best part of the whole process.

My mother nodded. "First I need a pan, though. A bread pan. Would you find one for me, please?"

Instead of the regular cake pan Mom used for other cakes, she put the marble cake in a bread pan.

While I rummaged around in the cupboard, my mother reached to the shelf above her and brought down a small mixing bowl. I set the bread pan on the counter. My mother started to pour some of the cake batter into the smaller bowl.

Not wanting to miss one moment of the next part, I positioned myself close to her elbow. She measured out the cocoa, added a little more milk and then took a spoon from the drawer.

"Would you hold the bowl for me, please?" she asked.

The bigger bowl had pretty much stayed where it belonged while my mother used the mixer, but stirring something in a small bowl was another task that required two hands, one to hold the bowl and one to mix. Unless she sat at the table. Then she could do it by herself.

While Mom grasped the counter with one hand and mixed the chocolate batter with the other, I held onto the bowl.

"There," she said, dipping the spoon up and down a couple of times, "that should be all right."

She pushed the small bowl out of the way.

"I suppose we'd better put a little shortening in the pan, too, just to be sure it won't stick," she said. "Would you do that?"

Like she had to ask. Being allowed to use the little brush she had bought from the Fuller Brush man was almost as much fun as helping Dad paint a hay wagon or the little round white granary where he stored soybeans. The brush had a silver sliding part that went down over the bristles to hold them together. I happily dabbed the brush into the open can of shortening.

When I had finished brushing the pan with shortening, I set it in front of my mother. She poured the yellow batter into it, and while I held the bowl over the pan, she scraped out the rest.

We repeated the process to put the chocolate mixture over the top.

Then I moved closer still so my nose was practically right over her hand. Now came the *very best* part.

"How do you know when you've mixed it enough?" I asked, as my mother pulled open the drawer and took out a butter knife.

"Hmmmm...I guess I've never thought about it," she said as she dipped the knife into the chocolate batter and started making back and forth, swirling movements. "But you have to be careful you don't mix it too much, otherwise you'll just end up with a very light chocolate cake...there," she said, ending with a flourish. She held the knife toward me.

Licking off the knife was the second-best part of making a marble cake. Not only did the cake end up marbled with chocolate, but the knife did, too.

My mother put the pan in the oven and set the timer.

"You're supposed to pre-heat so it warms up before you bake something, but I think it wastes electricity. And I haven't noticed it makes much difference to what you are baking," Mom said, as she turned on the oven.

"Now all we have to do is wait," she said, reaching for her crutches.

Ah, yes. The waiting. While we were mixing the cake and preparing the marble, the minutes had ticked by quickly. But now that the cake was in the oven, time seemed to slow down again.

My mother went back to her chair next to the picture window and started working on an embroidery project while I tried to concentrate on reading my book about Katie John.

In a little while, I could smell the cake baking in the oven, and then I found myself reading whole paragraphs a second time. It seemed to me Mom's marble cake smelled as good as the pale yellow roses that bloomed in the front lawn during the summer.

After what seemed like hours, the oven timer went off. I threw down my book, dashed out to the kitchen and waited impatiently until my mother arrived. It took her several minutes to get up and make her way to the kitchen. Finally, she set her crutches against the table and, grasping the stove with one hand, pulled open the oven door with the other. Using her free hand, she reached inside to pat the top of the cake with one finger.

Satisfied that the cake was done, Mom reached into the oven with a hot pad and pulled the pan toward the front. With one hand, she took it out of the oven and set it on another hot pad she had placed on the counter.

"How long until it cools off?" I asked.

Mom glanced at the kitchen clock. "Oh, in a half an hour it ought to be ready to cut."

I looked at the clock, too. In a half an hour, it would almost be time for supper.

She must have known what I was thinking.

"I know it won't be long until supper, but we haven't had marble cake in a long time, either." She smiled. "But only if you *promise* not to let it spoil your supper."

"I promise, cross my heart and hope to die. It won't spoil my supper. I'm sure it won't."

Which really was not an empty promise. Very few things affected my appetite. Not even a piece of cake shortly before mealtime.

While the cake was cooling, we went back into the living room. My mother began working on her embroidery project again. But instead of trying to concentrate on my book, I picked up one of my sister's magazines, although I don't know why. Makeup tips and hair care suggestions were not very interesting. I would rather read about cows or cats or dogs or horses.

Just when I thought I could not stand it another moment, Mom announced that the cake was cool enough to cut. We went out to the kitchen again, and I stood by mother's elbow and watched as she sliced into the marble cake.

"Are you *sure* this won't spoil your supper?" she asked, reaching into the cupboard for a small dessert plate.

"I'm sure."

Mom smiled. "No, I didn't think so."

I sat down at the table and admired my piece of marble cake. It was so pretty with all the swirls of chocolate laced through and through.

When I took the first bite, I found out the cake tasted every bit as good as it looked.

"How is it?" Mom asked.

"Yu-ummmmm-mmmeee!" I said.

"Good. I guess that means I haven't forgotten how to make a marble cake, then."

I paused before taking another bite. "Mom? How come you never use a recipe when you bake a cake?"

For all the years I had watched my mother bake cakes, I had never seen her use a recipe. Not once. Not for marble. And not for white, yellow, chocolate or pineapple upside-down.

She shrugged and tapped her temple. "It's all up here. I'm too lazy to get out the cookbook. Memorizing the ingredients seems easier."

The image of the half page I had to memorize for the Sunday school Christmas program popped into my head.

"How could memorizing be easier?"

"We used to have to do a lot of memorizing in school," Mom said as she cut off a bite of cake with her fork. "You get used to it after a while."

"You do?"

"Yes, you do."

Well, maybe my mother got used to memorizing. But I knew I was going to have nightmares about that half page until the Sunday school Christmas program was over. At least with a recipe, you did not have to say it out loud in front of a whole church-full of people.

"I will help you memorize your part for the Christmas program, if that's what's bothering you," Mom said. "When we're finished, you'll know it backwards and forwards. You'll be able to say it in your sleep."

To tell you the truth—that's exactly what I was afraid of.

****

~ 3 ~
HopAlong Cassidy

The next to the last cow hurried into the barn and into her stanchion. Outside, the gray afternoon light of a cloudy day was fading quickly and soon it would be dark. Over the last month, it had rained a couple of times, and not long ago, it had rained for two days straight. The barnyard was a muddy, mucky mess that I avoided if at all possible.

I walked toward the other end of the barn, watching the door, waiting for the last cow. The barn was filled with the jingling of stanchions as the cows stretched their necks to reach more of the ground corn and oats in front of them. I always thought the cow feed smelled so good, like a warm summer day with molasses mixed into it.

A minute went by, but the cow still had not appeared in the doorway. I crossed the gutter channel and walked toward my father, who was up in front of the cows, shutting the stanchions.

"Where's Patches?" I said.

Dad paused to look around. "Didn't she come in?"

"No, Daddy," I said.

"Maybe she's getting a drink," Dad suggested.

Sometimes one or two of the cows would linger by the stock tank for a few more sips, pushing their noses into the cold water and then lifting their heads while water dripped from their mouths. But the cows did that in the summer when it was hot outside, not during the fall when it was cold and almost dark by five o'clock. There wasn't much pasture for the cows to eat at this time of the year, and they knew that once they finished their feed, they would get some hay. They were eager to come into the warm barn now. Dad said it was a good idea to step back out of the way when I opened the door to let the cows in so I would not get run over.

My father looked toward the other end of the barn again where the yellow light from the overhead bulbs pushed out into the dark.

But still no Patches.

"Why don't you go out and see where she is. You've got your boots on, don't you?" Dad said.

I had put on my rubber chore boots before I left the house. Walking through the barnyard was like trying to walk through quicksand. Not that I actually knew what it was like to walk through quicksand. But the mud sucking at my boots, threatening to pull them off my feet with each step, seemed like what I would imagine quicksand would be.

If it had been any other cow, I would have asked Dad if we could wait for a few minutes to see if she would come in on her own. But Patches, and her sister, Rags, were special. They were not identical twins. One was "black on white" and the other was "white on black." I had never seen twin heifers before, and I had spent many evenings in the calf pen with them when they were babies combing the ends of their tails and brushing them with Dusty's soft brush while I waited for more milk to carry out to the milkhouse.

Rags and Patches had even gotten sponge baths with a kitchen sponge my mother had said I could take out to the barn. The sponge was yellow and old and ready to fall apart, but it worked just fine for sponging off Rags and Patches. I would put warm water in a calf pail, and then I would add a few drops of the lilac bubble bath Dad had given me for Christmas one year.

It was a whole lot more fun to give Rags and Patches a lilac sponge bath than it was to take a bubble bath myself. Dad said I had to make sure I squeezed most of the water out of the sponge so Rags and Patches would not get too wet.

Of course, Dad also said calves did not need sponge baths.

"Even if you were taking them to the fair, they wouldn't need to smell like lilacs," he'd said one night, wrinkling his nose.

My father liked the smell of lilacs as well as anyone. On a warm spring evening when the lilacs were in bloom, Dad and I would go out to the yard behind the house after the chores were finished to admire them. My grandmother, Inga, had planted the bushes at the time of the Great Depression, and they were now much taller than Dad. When the lilac bushes were heavy with blooms, the smell carried all the way across the yard.

I concluded that calves smelling like lilacs and lilac bushes smelling like lilacs must be different, as far as Dad was concerned.

After I had finished sponging off the calves, I used to wash their feet, too. At first, Rags and Patches were not too sure about standing with their foot in the bucket, but after a while they had grown used to it.

I walked to the end of the barn and out onto the concrete slab. It wasn't actually as dark outside as it had looked while I was in the barn. I reached the end of the concrete slab in front of the door, stopped, and carefully put one foot into the mud. I sank down to my ankle.

I took another step. And another. And with each step, the mud splashed and slurped and gurgled as I tried to pull my foot free. Finally I made my way around the corner of the barn.

And there was Patches.

"What are you doing out here?" I said. "How come you didn't come in?"

Patches stood holding up her right front foot, and when I talked to her, she took a couple hopping steps toward me. She gingerly put down her front foot but then quickly picked it up again.

And then I knew why Patches had not come into the barn.

She was lame.

"Wait here, Patches. I'll go and get Dad," I said.

I turned and hurried back to the barn as quickly as I could without losing my boots in the deep, squelching mud. My black rubber boots were muddy all the way up above my ankles, and I was glad that I had tucked my pant legs inside. Dad said if I did that, then the hems of my pants would stay clean. Mom thought it was a great idea. She said it took too much time to scrub the hems with a scrub brush and soap before she washed the pants. Dad said he did not know what difference it made. Mom said what was the use of washing clothes if they weren't clean by the time you were finished.

When I reached the barn, I stopped in the middle of the aisle and looked around. I couldn't see Dad anywhere. The cows were peacefully licking up the last of their feed, but I knew if I started shouting—in case Dad was in the haymow—they would get nervous. Most of the Holsteins would get nervous, anyway. The little Jersey cow we called Jersey and the several Guernseys in the herd wouldn't even notice if I started yelling.

Just then I spotted Dad up in front of the cows with the push broom, sweeping in the feed they had nudged out of reach with their rough, sandpapery tongues.

I turned and stepped over the gutter channel.

"Daddy! Patches is hurt," I said.

My father stopped sweeping. As usual, he was wearing blue denim work overalls, a denim chore jacket and a blue-and-white-pin-striped cap.

"Hurt?" he said. "What's wrong with her?"

"I don't know, but she's going on three."

The expression of concern in Dad's sky blue eyes turned to alarm.

"Going on three? Jeepers, I hope she didn't break her leg. You'd better show me where she is," he said.

My father set the handle of the push broom against the cement block wall and followed me to the door opening into the barnyard.

By now, Patches had come closer to the barn. She stood on the muddy cement, holding her leg up. In the light from the doorway, I could see a faint vapor of steam drifting up from her back, as if it had been very hard work to get this far.

"Patches—what have you done to yourself?" Dad asked.

"Moooooo-ooo," Patches said, low in her throat. She stretched her nose toward Dad.

"Let's see if we can get you in the barn," he said.

Dad put his hand on Patches' shoulder. "Take your time. We're not in any hurry." He turned to me. "Why don't you get behind her. Push on her rump. But not too hard. We don't want her to think she has to rush."

While I pushed on her rump, and while Dad nudged her shoulder, Patches took a hopping step forward and then another and another.

A few minutes later, the black and white cow carefully hopped through the door and into the barn. She stopped. We let her rest, and then we continued on toward her stall.

The other cows had finished eating their feed, and many of them turned their heads, stanchions jingling, to watch Patches as she continued her slow hopping progress down the barn aisle.

"Moooo," said Patches, when she saw her sister, Rags.

"Moooo-aaaaaa," Rags replied.

Most of the cows went into the same stalls each time. Rags and Patches, when we had started putting them in the stanchions as heifers, had ended up in different areas of the barn. When they were outside, they often stood together and grazed together and settled down in the soft pasture grass for naps together. When one came in the barn ahead of the other, they would often call a soft greeting to each other.

"Come on, Patches," Dad said, still walking beside the cow with his hand resting on her shoulder. "We're almost there."

In a few steps, we had arrived at Patches' stall. The black and white cow stood there for a few seconds, then she gathered herself and managed to hop over the gutter channel on three legs instead of using all four.

Dad squeezed beside her and reached for the stanchion to close it. He stepped back and looked down at her foot.

Although Patches' foot was flat on the straw, you could tell she was leaning in the other direction to take some of the weight off it. My father knelt beside her and pulled the golden straw away so he could see her foot better.

"Get some water in a calf pail, will you?" he said, looking over his shoulder at me.

I did as he asked, and when I handed the bucket to him, he splashed water on the top of Patches' foot. Because the barnyard was so muddy, you couldn't see her foot, only the mud that covered it.

Dad whistled softly through his teeth. "Oh, so that's it," he said. "Come and look at this.

I stepped across the gutter channel into the stall beside Dad and looked down at Patches' leg. Where the two sections of her cloven hoof met, the cow's foot was red and swollen. Because her foot was white, you could really see how red the skin was.

Dad reached down and gently touched the cow's foot.

Patches flinched and turned her head to look at us.

"Sore, isn't it," he said.

Dad gently touched the foot again. "She's probably got an infection of some kind. It's been so wet and cold this fall, I'm surprised they don't all have infected feet."

Once I had gotten an infection from a sliver in my finger. Every time I bumped that finger, it felt as if someone was poking it with a hot needle. But my finger had not looked as bad as Patches' foot.

"Daddy, Patches isn't going to die, is she?"

The very thought made a huge lump rise in my throat.

"No," Dad said, "she isn't going to die. Not from a sore foot. At least I hope not.

He stood there for a minute with his hand on the cow's back, patting her. Finally he turned to me.

"Go to the milkhouse and get pail of warm water. Not hot. But nice and warm."

"What are we going to do with a pail of water?"

"We're going to put some disinfectant in it, and then we're going to soak her foot," Dad explained.

"Is that going to help the infection?" I asked.

My father nodded. "I'm hoping the warm water will bring it to a head so it can drain. The disinfectant will keep the infection from getting worse."

"When will it start draining?"

Dad shrugged. "Maybe a day or two."

I stepped over the gutter channel. Some of barn cats had gathered in the middle of the barn aisle behind Patches' stall and were sitting with their tails curled around their front paws, watching us. That was one thing I had noticed about cats. Whenever you were doing something and turned around, there was often a cat or two or three sitting there watching.

One of the cats stood up and stretched and yawned. As she yawned, her ears went flat back on her head and then popped upright again. Most of our barn cats were brown tabbies. "Tiger cats" we called them.

The cats turned their attention back to Dad. Our dog, Needles, was sitting in the middle of the barn aisle too. He stayed out of the way while the cows came in the barn because some of them would chase him if they got the chance. Dad said cows were just naturally wary of dogs and that it had nothing to do with Needles himself. When the cows were in their stanchions, then Needles felt safe to wander around the barn. He never went up in front of the cows by the manger, though. The same cows who would try to chase him would lunge forward at him when he walked by.

"I'm going to get some warm water, Needles," I said.

The dog looked up at me with his round, brown eyes. His feathery tail was stretched out behind him. As he slowly wagged it back and forth, I could see that it was brushing clear a little spot in the white barn lime Dad had sprinkled on the floor. The barn lime smelled like chalk dust, it seemed to me.

By the time I returned with the pail of warm water, my father had retrieved the gallon jug of the iodine solution that he used when he washed the cows' udders before milking. Dad kept the gallon jug on the shelf by the milker pump.

My father put his finger into the bucket and nodded. "That's just right. Warm but not hot."

As soon as he began to pour the disinfectant into the water, I could smell the iodine. It was a sharp odor, somewhat like road tar under a hot summer sun. Dad said the iodine killed germs on the cows' udders. I knew it was important to kill germs before Dad put the milking machine on the cows so we would not end up with bacteria in our milk. We had learned about germs in science class at school. Germs could make you sick.

Maybe Dad was right. If the iodine solution could kill germs on the cows' udders, maybe it would kill the germs that were making Patches lame.

Dad stepped over the gutter channel and set the bucket by Patches' foot.

"Now, if we can get her to stand here for a while with her foot in the pail, it might help," Dad said.

My father gently picked up Patches' leg, pushed the pail into a better position and set her foot in the warm water.

Patches promptly picked her foot up and held it up.

My father once again grasped Patches' foot and tried to put it in the pail.

But Patches did not want a thing to do with it.

After three or four attempts, Dad stood up straight.

"Patches," he said. "We're trying to help you. If you don't put your foot in the warm water, it's not going to help."

The cow looked at Dad, as if she understood that he was talking to her.

"Patches, don't you remember?" I said. "We used to do this when you were a baby. Don't you remember getting your feet washed?"

My father got a funny expression on his face. Not an expression that meant he was going to laugh, but an expression that meant he had just thought of something really interesting.

"That's *right*. You used to give Rags and Patches foot baths," he said.

He moved closer to the cow next door. "Why don't you try it," he said.

"Me?" I said.

Dad nodded. "Maybe she'll remember if you do it."

I squeezed in next to Patches. Standing this close to her, I could feel the heat of her body against my face. That was always one nice thing about doing the chores during the winter. The cows gave off plenty of heat so the barn felt warm most of the time. Except if it was twenty or thirty below outside, but then it didn't feel warm anywhere, other than next to the wood stove in the living room.

I leaned down and put my hands around the cow's ankle. I couldn't help but notice that Patches was whole lot bigger now than she was the last time I had put her foot in a pail.

"Come on, Patches. Will you pick your foot up for me?" I said.

At first I did not think the black and white cow was going to lift her foot. But gradually I felt her body shift away from me as she eased her weight onto the other front hoof.

"Good girl," I said.

Slowly I put Patches' foot in the bucket with disinfectant in it.

But when the cow's toe touched the water, she quickly lifted her foot and pulled it out of the bucket.

"Almost. We almost did it," I said, as I began to move her foot back toward the bucket. The second time Patches did not flinch. Her foot went deeper into the warm water and then settled on the bottom of the pail.

"Well, look at that," Dad said softly. "I think she's going to let you soak her foot."

The black and white cow looked at me for a few seconds before she turned her attention to the pile of ground feed in front of her.

Dad laughed. "Cows won't eat if something is bothering them. Maybe the warm water feels good on her sore foot."

"How long should we let it soak?" I asked

"Until the water starts cool off, I suppose."

"How long will that be?"

"Hmmm, I don't know. Maybe 10 or 15 minutes. Somebody is going to have to stand here, though, to make sure she doesn't tip the bucket over."

Just then, I got a brilliant idea.

"I know!" I said. "I can get Dusty's brush, and while Patches' foot is soaking, I can brush her."

Dad smiled. "I think Patches would enjoy that."

My father stayed with the cow while I went to get Dusty's brush. During the summer I had kept my currycomb and brush in the machine shed. Dad said I could use the door track as a place to tie Dusty when I wanted to brush her. But now that the weather was colder, I had put my brush and curry comb in the barn and kept them on the little shelf next to the milker pump. When it was cold and windy outside, I would bring Dusty into the warm barn so I could tie her to one of the support posts.

"Here now," Dad said as I stepped across the gutter channel. "You have to keep your foot in the bucket for a while longer yet."

Patches had shifted her weight to her good foot again and looked as if she were going to pull her foot out of the bucket.

"Look Patches," I said. "I brought the brush. See?" I held up the brush.

I began to brush the cow's shoulder. As the soft brush swept over Patches, the cow relaxed and kept her foot in the bucket.

"Okay. Now that you're back, I'm going to throw down some hay for the cows," Dad said.

I slowly brushed Patches' neck and shoulder and flank. But I stayed away from her leg. I did not want Patches to get any ideas again about pulling her foot out of the bucket. As I brushed, I heard *thump-thump* as hay bales landed on the concrete in front of the manger when Dad tossed them through the door in the ceiling. If it was very cold, Dad kept the sliding doors shut over the hay holes, although the rest of the year, the doors stayed open. There were two doors in the ceiling, one on each side of the barn.

By the time I reached Patches' hip, I thought I should check the bucket and discovered the water was lukewarm.

"Daddy, will you come and check the water?" I said.

My father was shaking out a bale of hay for the cows on this side of the barn.

"Is it cold?" he asked, pausing with a flake of hay in his hands.

I shook my head. "No, but almost."

Dad tossed the flake of hay down for the cow in front of him. He reached into the watch pocket of his overalls, looked at his watch and put it back.

"Her foot's been soaking about fifteen minutes now. I think that's good enough," he said.

I set Dusty's brush down on the straw and lifted Patches' foot out of the bucket, and while I held her ankle with one hand, I pulled the bucket out of the way with the other. When I let go of Patches, she carefully set her foot on the straw.

"Does it look any better?" Dad asked as he crossed the gutter channel.

He turned his attention to the cow's foot. "You know, I think it doesn't look as red as it did before."

I could not be certain, but maybe the space between her toes was not *quite* as red.

"If we can soak her foot three times a day—morning, when we feed at night, and then just before we go in the house when we're done milking—it might really help her," Dad said.

"Do you think so?" I asked.

"Only one way to find out," my father replied. "And if it helps, maybe we won't have to change her name to HopAlong Cassidy."

I picked up the bucket of water and Dusty's brush. "Who is HopAlong Cassidy?" I asked.

"A cowboy in the movies," Dad replied. "A long time ago. In the old days."

"Oh," I said.

"Take that to the milkhouse and dump it down the drain. Don't toss it outside," Dad said.

"Okay," I said.

Throwing water out the door was not a problem in the summer. The water drained away and dried up quickly. But in the winter, throwing water out the door could mean we'd have an icy spot that would stay there until spring. From personal experience, I knew it was no fun at all to step out of the barn, walk a few steps, and then fall down on a patch of ice that you couldn't see in the dark.

As I came closer to the barn door, I could my white rabbit, Thumper, in his cage on top of the calf pen wall, eyes closed, sound asleep. Needles had curled up on a burlap feed sack Dad put in the corner for him between the door and the calf pen. He was sound asleep, too.

Needles knew it was not yet time to go to the house. When we went to the house for supper, the dog would come with us and would wait outside the door until we had finished eating and were ready to milk the cows. Then he would come back to the barn with us. He did not like to stay in the barn when people were not in the barn.

After I poured the bucket of water down the drain in the milkhouse, I went back to the barn.

"Put that pail in the corner by the milker pump," Dad said. "That way you can use the same one tonight before we go in the house and we'll only have one calf pail that smells like disinfectant."

"What's wrong with the calf pail smelling like disinfectant?" I asked.

Dad looked at me and shrugged. "Would *you* want to drink out of a glass that smelled like disinfectant?"

I shook my head.

"The calves wouldn't either," he said.

We only had two calves so far, but I could see his point.

I set the pail in the corner by the milker pump so I would be able to tell it apart from the other calf pails.

And that's how it became my job to soak Patches' foot three times a day for the next week.

I didn't mind, though.

After that first time, Patches was willing to pick up her foot and put it in the pail and to keep it there until the water cooled off. And while her foot was soaking, I used Dusty's brush to brush her. Mom let me take an old comb from the house, too, so I could comb the end of her curlicue tail, like I used to do when she was a baby.

In a few days, the black and white cow stopped going on three, and by the end of the week, her foot looked normal again and she was able to walk without limping.

See? I always knew it was a good idea to give Rags and Patches foot baths when they were babies.

Even if Dad did say that calves should not smell like lilacs.

****

~ 4 ~
Who Said Life Was Fair?

Halfway up the hill one afternoon, right after I had passed the wild plum trees growing next to the spring, I looked toward the living room picture window. I always looked toward the window when I was nearly as far as the silver maple, because most days after I got off the school bus, my mother would be sitting in her chair. As soon as she caught sight of me she would wave, and I would wave back.

Today I was surprised to see that the window was empty.

"Where's Mom, Needles?" I asked.

Needles came down the bank from the front yard, his tail going in circles. He pushed his way through the tall brown grass, and then, when he came out on the driveway, looked up at me, tail still wagging.

"Did Mom and Dad go to town this afternoon?"

Sometimes in the afternoon when Dad had caught up on his work, he would take Mom to town to go grocery shopping or to the bank or on some other errand. Because of the polio, my mother could not drive, and if she wanted to go somewhere, she had to wait for Dad, Loretta or Ingman to take her.

Of course sometimes in the afternoon when I arrived home from school, Mom would be in the kitchen, frosting a cake or cutting up bread she had baked. I was always hungry when I got home from school.

"Maybe we've got cake or fresh bread today!" I said to Needles.

The dog, brown eyes glinting, stopped and sneezed. Not once but three times. If Needles were happy or excited, he would sneeze. It seemed to me that he really liked going back in the field with Dad or over to our other place, because whenever Dad got in the pickup and then asked Needles if he wanted to come along, he would sneeze four or five times.

"If Mom made bread, I'll save some crust for you," I said.

Needles liked bread crusts, especially if the crust had a bit of butter on it.

Often I would climb the steep bank to the lawn, but I today I kept walking up the driveway. The ground wasn't frozen yet, but Dad said it would be soon. In few minutes, with Needles right beside me, I had almost reached the house.

"If there's bread, I'll bring out the crust in a little while," I said.

As I started up the steps to the porch, Needles turned and went to the little garage where Dad parked the car. I turned to look at the dog before I opened the door. Needles laid down by the garage, chin resting on his paws. The sun was shining there and he was out of the wind. I could also see that the car was in the garage, so that meant Mom and Dad had not gone anywhere.

Once I was inside the porch, I knew that my mother had not baked bread or cake. The smell of baking from the kitchen always filled the little porch, too. But I could not smell anything.

I opened the door leading into the kitchen.

The kitchen was empty.

"Mom?" I called, unzipping my coat. "Where are you? Mom?"

I expected my mother to answer from somewhere downstairs, either the living room or the bedroom. But instead of my mother's voice, I heard what sounded like a sneeze.

I took my coat off and started to hang it up on the back of a chair. Then I remembered Mom wanted me to hang my school coat in the closet as soon as I got home. She said it was easier that way. What I think she really meant is that if I hung my coat up right away, she wouldn't have to keep reminding me.

I turned toward the little closet between the kitchen and the bathroom and heard that sneezing sound again.

"Mom?" I said. "Is that you?"

"Yes, sweetheart. I'm right here," my mother said. Her voice sounded muffled.

I looked through the bedroom door. Mom was lying in bed on her back with the covers pulled up to her chin, underneath the white bedspread with knobby flower patterns on it. Loretta said that kind of bedspread was something called chenille.

"Hang your coat up," my mother said.

I slid open the closet door, hung up my coat and went into the bedroom.

"What's the matter? Are you sick?" I said.

She struggled to sit up. "Oh, it's nothing, really. Just a little ...just a little...a...a...a... a-CHOO!"

"A cold?" I said. "You caught a cold?

My mother nodded. "Yes, I've got a cold."

Except that it sounded like, "Yeth, ah've got a code."

"Have you been under the covers all afternoon?" I asked.

"Pretty much," Mom said. "Right after I finished the dinner dishes, I was so cold, I just could not get warm. I put more wood in the woodstove, but it didn't seem to help. So I thought it might be best to get under the blankets."

"Are you still cold? Do you want me to get some more blankets?"

Mom shook her head. "I feel better now. Dad came in a couple of times this afternoon and put more wood in the stove. He turned the furnace up, too. With heat coming in from both sides, it wasn't long before it felt a little warmer in here."

The furnace grate in the kitchen was right next to the closet in the hallway. Mom and Dad's bedroom had two doors: one on the side of the room closest to the bathroom and one opening into the living room. One time my mother had told me that the bedroom used to be the living room, and when it was the living room, the door was a window. The living room we had now had been built not long after I was born.

It seemed impossible to me that Mom and Dad's bedroom had once been a living room.

My mother sniffled. "I've been trying to think ... to think—a...a...a...CHOO!"

She rubbed the tip of her nose. "I've been trying to think about what we should have for supper. Maybe you could—a...a...a...CHOO!"

Mom sniffled again.

"Should I get a box of Kleenex?" I asked.

"Oh, would you please? I wasn't sneezing this much before, otherwise I would have brought one in here with me or had your dad get one for me."

"I'll be right back," I said.

From plenty of personal experience, I knew colds were not to be taken lightly. First you felt a slight tickle in your nose. Then you began sneezing. After that, you found yourself blowing your nose every two minutes. And in no time flat, you couldn't breathe through your nose and it was so sore, you wanted to cry at the thought of touching it. Not to mention that it was nearly as red as the radishes Dad grew in the garden every summer.

And that was only on the first day. You still had at least a week, or maybe even two weeks, before you could hope to feel better. And another week after that before the painful cracks on your nose started to heal up.

I went out to the kitchen to get the box of Kleenex sitting on the counter by the copper canisters.

Well, it was not actually Kleenex. It was Puffs. We kept two kinds of tissues for blowing your nose. The Puffs were nice and soft and helped your nose not to be so sore.

As far as I was concerned, whoever had invented Puffs was a very smart person.

I walked into the bedroom and held out the box.

"Here's the Puffs, Mom," I said.

My mother looked at me and shook her head. Her slate blue eyes were puffy and a little watery.

"Oh, no. That's all right," she said. "Get the other box."

For just a second there, I thought she said I should get the other box.

"What?" I asked.

"Get the other box."

"The *other* box?"

"Yes, the other box."

"But," I said. "Don't you want the Puffs?"

I held the box toward her.

Mom shook her head. "No, that's all right. Get the other box."

"But Mom. The other ones are like blowing your nose ... well ... like blowing your nose on a piece of plywood!"

"No, they aren't," Mom said.

"Yes, they are."

"No, they're not."

"Yes, they are."

"No they aren't. You're exaggerating again."

It came out sounding like "yer egg-as-erating agid."

"I am not!"

"Get the other box," Mom said.

"But they'll make your nose sore."

"No, they won't."

"Yes, they will."

"No, they won't."

"They will!"

My mother gazed at me, her blue eyes turning steely. "Get the other box. I want to save the Puffs in case you need them."

"Why would I need them? I'm not sneezing!"

"Not now, you're not," my mother agreed. "And I sure hope you don't catch this. But you never know. Now go and get the other box."

I looked at her for a few moments.

"Oh, all right. But you'll be sorry," I said.

"No, I won't."

"Yes, you will."

Mom shook her head, and from the look in her eyes, I knew I had better go and get the box of Kleenex."

I went back out to the kitchen.

"Here you are," I said, setting the box on the bed where Mom could reach them. "But you'll be sorry."

My mother smiled. "No I won't."

"What makes you so sure?" I asked.

Mom shrugged. "I just know," she said. "Now go and wash your hands. And do a good job."

"Why?"

"Just in case you picked up any of my germs. Maybe if you wash your hands often, and I wash my hands often, we can keep you from catching this. You always get so sick when you've caught a cold."

She could say that again.

"Okay," I said.

"And when you're finished with that, I want you to get some potatoes from the basement and peel them. There's leftover roast in the refrigerator from the other day. Dad can make hash for supper."

"Dad knows how to make hash?"

"Of course. He did all the cooking when I was in the hospital for six months. He took care of your brother and sister, too, and my dad."

I knew my mother had been stricken with polio in November and was taken to a hospital two hundred and fifty miles away. And I knew my brother and sister had been five years old and three years old at the time. But I guess I had never really thought about who had done the cooking while she was gone.

As I went into the bathroom to wash my hands, I could not stop thinking about the Kleenex. I had always heard that mothers made extreme sacrifices for their children (after all, if my mother said so, it must be true), but this seemed to be carrying it a bit too far. I figured by the next morning after using those awful cardboardy tissues instead of the wonderfully soft Puffs, Mom's nose would be sore and cracked and maybe even ready to fall off her face.

The next morning while I was upstairs getting dressed to go out to the barn to help Dad before I got ready for school, I kept listening for the sound of sneezing. But I could not hear a thing.

When I went downstairs, my mother was sitting on a chair by her end of the table with a cup of coffee in front of her.

"How is your nose?" I asked.

"My nose?"

"Is it sore yet?"

"My nose is fine," Mom said. "I'm fine. My cold is gone."

I felt my eyes narrow.

"Gone?" I asked. "How can it be gone? You only got sick yesterday."

Mom shrugged. "Well … that's the way my colds always are. Haven't had one in years, though."

Now that she mentioned it, I realized I had never seen my mother with a cold.

"But," I spluttered, "how can it be gone. I always get so sick—and you got better in one day?"

"It was just a little cold," Mom said. "Nothing serious."

"But, it's … that's… well …it's … it's… NOT FAIR."

My mother smiled gently. "Now sweetheart, whoever told you life was supposed to be fair?"

Who, indeed…

****

~ 5 ~
Teacher's Pet

Before I opened the barn door to go inside, I stopped to look up at the stars. There was no moonlight, and tiny sparkles that seemed no bigger than the end of my finger filled the black sky overhead. In science class at school, we had learned that the stars we could see in the sky were just like the sun, except they were so far away, they looked small. I wondered if someone else somewhere else far away on another planet was, at this moment, looking up in the sky and seeing the sun from such a distance that it looked like a twinkly little star. Our teacher said the scientists said there was no other life in the universe. But with so many stars, how they could know for sure?

As I stood with my head tilted back, the stars began to look blurry. It was the beginning of November, and a wind strong enough to make my eyes water blew out of the north. I wiped the tears out of my eyes, reached for the latch on the barn door and went inside.

Even from the porch steps, I had been able to hear the steady humming of the milker pump. Dad and Ingman were already milking cows. We had finished eating supper a short while ago, and then I had helped Mom with the dishes. Ingman was working the seven-to-three shift at the creamery in town, so he could help Dad milk. My job would involve carrying milk to the milkhouse and feeding the calves when the milking was finished.

In the corner between the door and calf pen, the barn cats lapped milk out of a dish. A few feet away, Needles sat watching them. He was waiting for the cats to finish so he could lick out the dish. Needles liked the cats, and the cats liked Needles. It's just that we had so many barn cats there wasn't room for the dog to get to the dish.

"Needles!" I said.

The cream-colored Cocker Spaniel and Spitz mix dog turned his head to look at me. Then he went back to watching the cats.

From where I stood by the door, I could see that Dad and Ingman were a third of the way through milking.

I walked down to talk to Dad.

"Do you want me to carry milk?" I asked.

My father crouched by a cow, getting ready to turn off the vacuum and remove the milker. He shook his head.

"No, that's okay. We can get it," he said.

If Dad was milking by himself, then it was my job to carry all of the milk to milkhouse and dump it into the bulk tank. When the milker bucket was only half full, I could carry it. But if the bucket was more than half full, I had to dump it into the milk pail and carry the pail to the milkhouse. Most of the time I used the milk pail, though, no matter whether the milker bucket was full. That way, if Dad needed the extra milker bucket before I got back, he would have it for the next cow.

Dad stepped over the gutter channel and set the milker bucket on the floor with a thump. The stainless steel sleeves around the inflations tinkled and clanked against the bucket.

"Are you sure you don't want me to carry milk?" I asked

Dad shook his head. "We can do it," he said. "When we get down to the end, then you can feed the calves."

"Okay, Dad," I said.

I was hoping that's what he would say. Now I would have time to teach Needles a new trick.

I turned and walked back toward the other end of the barn. The kitties had finished lapping up milk, giving Needles an opportunity to lick out the dish.

"Let's work on our new trick, Needles," I said.

The dog paused, looked up at me and then went back to licking out the already spotless dish. The kitties drank their milk out of an old stainless steel frying pan that had lost its handle. Whenever Ingman washed the milkers, he scrubbed out the cat dish, too, even if it did not need to be scrubbed. The pan was so shiny it looked brand new.

The wooden milk stool, with edges worn to a rounded smoothness from years of use, sat in the corner by the calf pen. Dad and Ingman did not use the milk stool every time they milked. And Dad used it more than Ingman, especially if he was milking a cow who was touchy about the milker and he had to keep a careful eye on her.

I picked up the milk stool and moved it closer to the cat dish. Needles already knew "sit" and "stay," but now I wanted to teach him something new.

"Come here, Needles," I said.

The dog wagged his tail, his brown eyes bright.

I patted the milk stool. "Come here, Needles," I said.

With a questioning look in his eyes, Needles approached the milk stool and sniffed the top, his nose going from side to side. I patted the stool again. "Hop up here."

The dog put one paw on the stool but then changed his mind. The milk stool was not very big, certainly not as big as the bed of the pickup truck or a hay wagon. But Needles could jump in the back of the truck or onto the hay wagon with a single, easy leap, so I was sure he could get up on the milk stool.

"Try again. Come here," I said, patting the milk stool.

This time, Needles put both paws up on the edge. But once again he changed his mind.

I patted the stool. "You can do it. I know you can."

Needles put both paws on the stool and stood there. I could tell he was thinking about what he should do next. Slowly, carefully, he raised one hind leg and set his paw on the edge of the stool.

"Good boy!" I said.

Needles stood with three legs on the stool and one on the floor for many long seconds. Then he carefully raised the last foot and stood on the edge of the stool, teetering.

All at once he leaped forward, sending the milk stool backwards with a crash.

"Trying to teach Needles a new trick, are you," Dad said as he paused by the cat dish with a full bucket of milk. The barn cats crowded around him.

"Yes," I said.

"Be patient. It's gonna take him a while to figure out what you want," Dad said.

"I know, Daddy," I said.

Mom had told me many times that patience was not my "strong suit." Whatever that meant. But Needles had learned "sit" and "stay" so fast, I was sure he would quickly learn the new trick.

As Dad headed for the door with the full milker bucket, I patted the stool yet again.

"Come on, Needles!" I said.

The dog approached slowly. Once again, he climbed onto the stool.

And once again, with four paws balanced on the edge, he leaped forward and knocked the stool over.

I drew a deep breath and let it out slowly. Mom said you should always stop and count to ten when something was bothering you.

"Come on, Needles," I said. "You have to get up on the milk stool before we can start working on our new trick."

The dog looked up at me and then at the milk stool. Up at me. And then at the stool.

After a while, he got up on the stool once more with all four paws.

"Bring your feet forward a little, Needles," I said.

I pulled one of Needles' paws forward and then the other one.

"See?" I said. 'It's not so bad. Now for the next part."

I put my hand on Needles' back near his tail.

"Sit!" I cried. "Sit!"

The dog's ears quivered, but nothing else moved.

"Sit!" I said.

Needles leaped forward, and once again the milk stool crashed to the floor.

As I set the milk stool upright, Dad came back in the barn.

"Still at it, I see," he said as he walked past.

I drew another deep breath and let it out slowly.

"Yes, Daddy," I said.

"Just make sure the stool doesn't fall on one of kitties if Needles tips it over again."

I glanced back at the cats. They were sitting in a row behind me and were nowhere near close enough for the stool to fall on them.

I patted the stool, and Needles looked at me, ears quivering. He took a hesitant step forward and then another one. He carefully placed his front paws on the edge and hopped up.

"Come on, Needles! A couple more steps! You can do it!" I said.

Needles slowly inched his front paws forward.

"Good boy! That's perfect!" I said.

Needles looked up at me. He still did not seem to be too sure about standing on the milk stool.

"That's good, Needles. Very good. Let's see if you can jump down without knocking it over," I said.

I patted my leg. Needles looked at me for a few seconds, then he gathered himself, leaped forward and landed on the barn floor next to me. The milk stool rocked back and forth, and for a second, I thought it would stay upright. Then it crashed to the floor.

"What in the world are you trying to do?" asked my big brother Ingman. He had a milker bucket in one hand. He stepped around the overturned milk stool so he could pour more milk in the cat dish.

The dish had already been filled several times, and most of the cats were not hungry anymore. They appeared to be more interested in watching Needles working on his new trick. The kitties liked the milk stool, too, and if Dad or Ingman needed it, the cats would wait until it was placed back in the middle of the barn aisle. And then one, or sometimes two of them, would sit on the stool to groom themselves.

Ingman, with the milker bucket in one hand, turned and looked at Needles. "Is she trying to teach you another trick?" he asked the dog.

Needles wagged his tail.

"Just remember," my big brother said to me. "The milk stool isn't a very big place for a dog. He might not want to stand on it."

"I know," I said. "I've already noticed that."

My brother grinned, showing his very white and very even teeth, then he turned and headed for the door.

I reached for the milk stool and set it upright.

"Here, Needles! Let's try it again!"

The dog was looking at me as if I had suddenly sprouted two heads. His ears were quivering, and his eyebrows were gathered into little bunches above his eyes, making him look as though he were frowning. Instead of wide sweeps of his tail, just the tip moved.

"Here, boy!" I said, patting the stool.

As if someone had tied an invisible rope to his collar and was pulling him along, the dog moved toward the milk stool. When I patted the seat, he looked up at me with worried eyes. Then he climbed up on the stool and inched his front paws forward.

This time the milk stool was not teetering.

"Good dog!" I said.

As Needles stood there, looking around him uncertainly, Ingman came back into the barn with the empty milker bucket.

"Hey!" he said. "You did it, Needles. Look at you."

He set the milker bucket down and then patted the dog on the head.

"You must be the teacher's pet, Needles!"

"Teacher's pet?" I said.

"You're the teacher. He's the pet," my big brother said.

"Hah, ha. Very funny," I said.

Ingman grinned, picked up the milker bucket and headed back to the milking.

I looked at Needles, and once again, just the tip of his tail wagged. When Needles wagged his tail like that, it meant he wanted to wag it but did not know if he should.

"It's okay, Needles," I said. "Very good."

Now that the dog had sure footing on the milk stool, I figured we could work on the rest of the trick. I put my hand on Needles' back once more.

"Sit!" I cried.

Needles had learned "sit" a long time ago. He would sit even if I was out in the yard and he was over by the shed. In fact, he would sit any time that I asked him to.

Except for now.

"Sit!"

Needles looked up at me and then stared straight ahead.

"Sit!" I said again, a little more forcefully. Maybe with the milker pump and the milkers running, he could not hear me as well.

"Sit! Sit, Needles!"

The dog still stared straight ahead, and then, without seeming to move very much, he leaped off the milk stool. This time, it did not crash to the floor.

"You're supposed to stay on the stool, Needles!" I said.

I patted the stool. "Come here!"

Needles took a step backward.

"Come here!"

I stomped my foot to give my words emphasis.

Needles took another step backward.

"Bad dog!" I said. "You're supposed to come here! What's wrong with you!"

"What," Dad said, "are you yelling about? You're upsetting the cows."

My father was carrying another milker bucket to the milk house.

"I'm not yelling," I said.

"Yes," Dad said, frowning. "You are."

"I am?"

He nodded and set the milker bucket on the floor.

Needles took one more look at me. He moved toward Dad, edged around behind my father's legs and peeked out at me, ears trembling. Even the whites of his eyes were showing a little bit.

"I want Needles to sit on the milk stool. But he won't!" I said.

"Of course he won't. Not if you yell at him," Dad replied.

"I'm not yelling!"

"Well, maybe you are and maybe you're not. But Needles *thinks* you are."

"I wanted to make sure he could hear me," I said.

"The dog is not deaf," Dad replied. "He can hear you."

"I thought with the milker pump and the milkers, maybe he couldn't hear me."

"He can hear you all right."

"Then why won't he sit?"

"Because he thinks you're yelling at him," Dad said.

"I am not! You don't think I'm yelling, do you, Needles?"

The dog's nose twitched. But it was all that moved. He did not come out from behind Dad's legs.

"Try not to be so loud," my father said. He picked up the milker bucket and headed for the door.

"Come here, Needles," I said.

The dog looked at Dad, glanced at me once, and then trotted to catch up with my father and followed him out of the barn.

I felt like stomping my foot again. Needles clearly did not want to stay in the barn with me.

I had never had a puppy before we got Needles. One year a neighbor's beagle had come to our farm and had stayed for a couple of months. He wasn't really a neighbor because the man lived quite a few miles away. The dog was in the habit of roaming around, and she would stay at one place and then the next as she traveled across the countryside. But that was the closest I had been to having a dog.

If Needles was not out in the field with Dad, he would wait on the front lawn underneath the big silver maple tree for me to come home from school. If I walked back in the pasture to bring the cows up to the barn, Needles would come with me. And whenever I took Dusty for a ride, Needles usually came with me then, too.

Maybe Dad was right. Maybe I *had* been louder than I thought. Sometimes Mom told me I did not need a telephone to talk to my best friend, Vicki, who lived a couple miles south of our place. She said all I would need to do is open the window and yell, and Vicki would be able to hear me just fine.

In a few minutes, my father returned to the barn, empty milker bucket in hand, with Needles right behind him.

"Now what's wrong?" Dad asked.

I had sat down on the milk stool and was wiping my eyes with a handkerchief I kept in my pocket. Mom had bought some handkerchiefs at the fall church bazaar on which someone had crocheted borders. The handkerchief smelled like roses because Mom had also bought some blue satin sachets she kept with the handkerchiefs.

"Needles doesn't like me anymore," I sniffled.

Dad sighed and set down the milker bucket. "He still likes you."

"No he doesn't. When you left, he wouldn't even stay here with meeeeeeee!" I wailed.

"I suppose he's afraid you'll holler at him again. He probably thinks *you* don't like *him*."

I looked at Dad and then at Needles, who had once again positioned himself behind my father's legs.

Could it be true? Did Needles really think I did not like him?

"Maybe you should tell him you're sorry," Dad suggested.

"Here, Needles," I said in a quavering voice. I patted my leg.

Needles looked at Dad.

"It's okay," Dad said, reaching for the milker bucket, "she's not mad at you anymore."

As my father walked back toward the cows, the dog crept forward, his tail held low to the ground.

"I'm sorry I yelled at you."

Needles sat down by the milk stool.

"I didn't mean to yell at you, honest."

Needles leaned toward me—and then he rested his chin on my knee.

A little while later, I stood up and patted the milk stool. Needles hopped up as if he had been doing it every day for the last month.

"Good boy!" I said. "I only want you to sit on the milk stool."

Needles looked up at me, cocked his ears and titled his head. He always did that when someone said something he was interested in hearing, such as "want to ride on the tractor, Needles?" The dog loved riding on the tractor. He would sit on the seat while Dad stood up to drive. Dad said since Needles like riding on the tractor so much, maybe he should teach the dog how to drive.

But what had I said to make Needles cock his ears and tilt his head?

"I want you to sit, but …"

I stopped in mid-sentence.

Needles was sitting on the milk stool, tail hanging over the edge, just the tip brushing the floor.

"You did it!" I said. "You did it!

"Well," Dad said, setting down another full milker bucket. "I see you and Needles have made up."

"Daddy, look! Needles is sitting on the milk stool."

The dog, his eyes bright and sparkly, began to pant, just the tip of his tongue showing from between his teeth. Needles panted like that when he was especially pleased with himself.

"Yup. He's sittin' on the milk stool," Dad said.

"Is that what all the yelling has been about?" Ingman asked. Dad and Ingman were nearly finished milking and had almost reached the last two cows on this end of the barn.

"I wasn't yelling," I said. "At least, I didn't mean to."

"Look at you, Needles," Ingman said. "You're sitting on the stool."

Needles looked back and forth between, Dad, Ingman and me and wagged his tail even harder.

Dad laughed. "That's a good trick, Needles."

"You look pretty important sitting there," Ingman said.

Dad turned back toward the cows. "We'd better finish milking. Then you can feed the calves," he said.

One of the milkers began to make a high-pitched whining sound.

"Oops. Better catch that," Ingman said. He quickly went to the cow to take the milker off before it fell off into the straw. If the milkers fell into the straw while the vacuum was still turned on, they sucked up straw into the milker bucket.

I knelt on the floor and put my arms around Needles. He turned his head, leaned into me, and with one single swipe of his tongue, licked my nose.

After that, whenever I pointed at the milk stool, Needles would hop up on it and sit down. I never had to say a word to him.

Dad and Ingman always laughed, too, when they saw Needles sitting on the milk stool.

After a while, my father began to wonder why I had not taught the dog to milk cows yet, seeing as Needles already knew how to sit on the milk stool.

Of course, I don't know why Dad wondered about that.

He had not taught Needles how to drive the tractor yet, either.

~ 6 ~
The Worst Picture

We were part way through supper one night when Dad asked the question that I had been dreading ever since the photographer had come to school more than a month ago. "Are your pictures back yet?" Dad said as he helped himself to another slice of homemade bread and started spreading butter on it.

When my father put butter on his bread, he meant business. Mom would only spread a thin layer of butter on her bread. Dad put on about as much butter as a slice of bread could hold.

"No, Dad," I said. "Our pictures aren't back yet."

It was only Mom, Dad and me at the table. Ingman was working at the creamery, and Loretta had already moved to the apartment she had rented for the winter. My sister always rented an apartment during the winter in the city where she worked at the electric cooperative so she would not have to drive thirty miles every day on slippery roads with her sea-green four-door V8 Chevrolet Bel-Air. Each weekend she came home on Friday night and then went back late Sunday afternoon.

For some reason that I could never figure out, Dad always asked for one of my school pictures to keep in his billfold. Every year, the packet of school pictures contained smaller wallet-sized photos and some larger wallet photos and a five-by-seven.

My father was not the type of person to go around showing pictures to people. My mother, yes. My sister, of course. My brother, maybe. But Dad? He milked cows, planted crops and fixed machinery. He just did not seem like the type of person who would want a picture.

Some of the girls at school really enjoyed having their pictures taken. They would spend many days talking about what they were going to wear and how they were going to fix their hair and whether their mothers were going to buy them a new dress or a new blouse, or at the very least, maybe some new barrettes. When it came time for the pictures, they would smile as if they were models, like the models in the women's magazines my sister subscribed to. When the pictures came back, they were lovely. Not a frown or a scowl anywhere.

And then there were those kids who, if they did not exactly enjoy getting their pictures taken, being photographed was no big deal. This group included both boys and girls. They would wear what they usually wore to school. And when they sat in front of the photographer's screen, they would smile a nice, normal smile and would go happily on their way when the pictures were finished.

And then there was me.

For me, getting my picture taken was a terrible experience. I knew it did not matter what I wore or how I combed my hair, because the pictures were going to turn out awful. They always did. When the photographer said "smile," my face froze, and I could not smile if my life depended on it.

That's what Mom said, that she could not do something if her life depended on it. Such as, "When that mouse ran over my foot, I couldn't have kept myself from screaming if my life depended on it." Which had happened once when my mother was standing by the sink washing the dishes. A mouse had scurried across the floor and over her foot. I was sitting by the table, finishing up some homework, and I almost jumped out of my skin when she screamed.

Sometimes we had lots of trouble with mice in our old farmhouse.

The photographer who took the pictures at school was a nice man who liked to laugh and tell jokes. Now and then he got creative and said something like, "repeat after me as fast as you can— 'rubber baby buggy bumpers ... rubber baby buggy bumpers ... rubber baby buggy bumpers...'"

If the photographer said something silly, all the other kids waiting in line started giggling, and then, so would I. Although, by the time I sat down in front of the screen, I was no longer giggling. Who could giggle in a situation like that? Certainly not me. Not with a camera pointing at me. But at least it was possible for me to smile. A little. Sometimes.

Nothing like that had happened this year. The photographer had said I should not look so serious, but no one had been giggling in line behind me, so smiling was out of the question.

But that wasn't the worst of it. No, the worst of it was that this was the first time I had been photographed wearing glasses.

It had all started at the beginning of the year when the teacher had done the eye tests. I was not sure what the direction of the "E" had to do with anything or whether I could read the bottom of the line on the chart. Mom said the eye tests showed if I could read my books or see the chalkboard. I'd never had a problem with it before, but according to the teacher, I needed to have my eyes checked by an eye doctor.

The next thing I knew, Mom had made an appointment. And when the appointment was nearly finished, the eye doctor told me I needed glasses. Mom said it was nothing to be upset about because she wore glasses, too, for reading.

But I did not have to wear my glasses only for reading. I had to wear them all the time. And none of the frames I had tried on seemed to make any difference. When I faced the mirror, they all made me look like I was peering out of a dark cave. Actually, that's what I felt like, too, as if I were peering out a dark cave. Or what I would imagine it would be like peering out of a dark cave.

And now Dad was wondering if my school pictures were back yet.

"No, Dad," I said once again, looking across the supper table at him, "I haven't seen any pictures so far."

"Should be soon, though," Mom said." Why don't you ask tomorrow?"

The next day at school, the last thing I wanted to do was ask about pictures. I kept putting it off and hoping someone else would ask. As morning turned to noon and noon turned into afternoon, I was still waiting. As we gathered up our books and papers at the end of the day, another girl finally spoke up. She was one of those who liked having her picture taken. The teacher told her that our pictures would be here on Friday.

"Did you find out about your pictures today?" Dad asked that night during supper.

"They're supposed to be here by the end of the week," I explained.

"Good," he said.

On Friday, as the buses were pulling up in the driveway outside of the school building, our teacher handed out the envelopes. The other kids immediately took out their pictures to admire them and to show them off to each other.

I carried the envelope with my name on it to my desk, opened the flap and cautiously peeked inside. Then I closed up the envelope as quickly as I could. Because we were almost ready to go home, no one asked about seeing my pictures.

Once we were on the bus, however, my best friend, Vicki, asked. She showed me her pictures first, and she looked like she did in person, with her short, light-brown hair and cheerful smile. After she put her pictures back in the envelope, I slowly pulled out one of mine.

"That's nice!" Vicki said.

I stared at her in disbelief as the bus rumbled along a back country road beside the river.

"Nice!" I said. "I look awful."

Vicki's eyebrows inched up on her forehead.

"What do you mean?"

"I look terrible. Those glasses..."

"What's wrong with them?" she asked.

"They make me look like ... well ... they make me look like ... a ... a ... raccoon. A raccoon in a cave! A sick raccoon in a cave!"

Vicki shook her head. "They do not! They're only glasses, that's all. And the picture is nice. It looks just like you."

The picture looked just like me?

Jeepers. It was worse than I thought.

Vicki handed the picture back, and I quickly put it in the envelope.

"You're too hard on yourself," Vicki said.

We rode along in silence for a few minutes.

"Do you think you can come over to my house on Sunday? Or should I come to yours?" Vicki asked.

On many weekends, either I went to Vicki's house or she came to mine. I had never had someone my own age live so close before. Vicki lived on a turkey farm a couple of miles from our dairy farm. During the summer we rode our bikes back and forth. Sometimes, too, I rode Dusty. When I was at Vicki's house, I helped her with her turkey chores, and when the chores were done, we would explore the woods or go fishing or pack a lunch and go for a bike ride.

When Vicki came to my house, she helped with cow chores or baling hay. When we were finished, we would explore the woods. And sometimes, if she were there on a summer evening, my big sister would take us to the root beer stand in town.

But we only rode our bikes back and forth during the summer. The weather was too cold now to ride bikes. Either Loretta would have to drive me to Vicki's house, or Vicki's dad would have to bring her to my house. Her mom did not drive. And because of the polio, my mom could not drive.

"I know," Vicki said. "I'll call you tomorrow morning, and then we can figure out if I'm going to your house or if you're coming to mine."

"Okay," I said.

The day had started out sunny, but as the bus headed back to the main road, I walked up the hill under a cloudy sky. I looked for Needles, but he was not waiting for me beneath the maple tree. I figured he was probably in the barn with Dad where it was warmer, and where he would soon be busy trying to stay out of the way as the cows came inside for their feed.

I could see my mother sitting by the living room window. As I came closer to the maple tree, she looked up and waved. I waved back.

By the time I walked into the kitchen, Mom had already picked up her crutches and was on her way from the living room.

"Did you get your pictures?" she asked.

"Yes," I said, setting my books on the table.

I went to the hall closet to hang up my coat, returned to the kitchen and sat down.

"Well?" Mom said.

"Well—what?" I asked.

"What about your pictures?"

"Do you want to see them?"

"Of course I want to see them!"

I pulled the envelope out of the folder where I had put it and held it out toward my mother. She opened the envelope and took out the 5 x 7 photograph.

"It's so nice!" Mom said. "You look like you always do."

Great. That was pretty much the same thing Vicki had said.

"Yes, I know. I look like I do in person."

"What's the matter? Don't you like your pictures?" Mom asked.

I shrugged and headed upstairs to change my clothes.

My sister arrived home for the weekend a little while later.

"Did you get your pictures yet?" she asked.

Without saying a word, I held out the envelope to her.

"Nice picture," she said. "That's a pretty color on you."

"I know. And I look just like I do all the time."

"What?" my sister said.

"Nothing," I said. "Never mind."

Dad waited until we were all sitting at the table to ask.

"Did you get your pictures today?"

"Yes, Daddy," I said.

"When we get done with supper will you get one for my billfold?" he asked.

"Get one for me, too, will you?" my sister said.

"What for?" I asked.

My mother cleared her throat. "If your sister wants a picture, get a picture for her. It's not polite to ask why."

"Yes, Mom," I said.

"I want to keep it in my jewelry box at my apartment," Loretta explained.

After supper, I cut out two of the wallet-sized photos and handed one to Dad.

My father gazed at the picture for a few moments. "I was supposed to get glasses once," he said.

He laid the picture on the table and reached for the pin on the front pocket of his blue chambray work shirt. I had noticed that other men kept their billfolds in their back pockets, but Dad kept his billfold in his front shirt pocket. If the buttonhole was loose so that the pocket would not stay closed very well, then he would pin it closed.

"You were supposed to get glasses?" I asked.

I had never seen Dad wear glasses—not even sun glasses. My father could thread fish line into the tiny eye of one of the tiny hooks we used for ice fishing. It did not seem to me that Dad needed glasses.

"Yes. Once upon a time, I was supposed to get glasses," Dad said.

"Why didn't you?" I asked as I handed the other picture to my sister.

Dad drew a breath as if he were going to say something. But then he stopped.

"What Daddy? What were you going to say?" I asked.

"I think you should tell her," Mom said.

As I sat there waiting for him to say something, a strange, haunted look came into Dad's blue eyes that I had never seen before.

"Well, I was just a little kid," he said. "It was during the winter, and we'd gotten a big snowstorm the day before."

I knew Dad had grown up in northern Wisconsin during the 1920s and that his mom and dad were cooks at a lumber camp.

"You didn't get glasses because there was too much snow?" I asked.

My father shook his head. "My dad thought I really needed glasses. He studied to be a doctor, you know. We were going to walk to town."

He stopped and began fiddling with his butter knife, flipping it from side to side.

"What happened?" I asked.

"We, ah, we… made it to the end of the driveway…"

"Then what?" I said.

"And then…he…collapsed."

"Your dad fell down because of all the snow?"

My father shook his head.

"He had a heart attack and died. Right there on the spot."

I stared at him, not knowing what to say.

"I was only a kid, and there wasn't a single thing I could do to help him," Dad continued. "He died right there in front of me."

By now, I had tears in my eyes. "Oh…Daddy…"

"Well," he said, "that was a long time ago. More years than I care to remember."

My sister got up and handed me a tissue. She got one for herself, too. And one for Mom.

"But you never got your glasses," I said, as I took off my glasses and laid them on the table. I wiped my eyes with the tissue. Mom blew her nose. And so did Loretta.

"No, I never got glasses. Didn't seem very important after that," he replied.

I could see what he meant.

"Thanks for the picture, kiddo," he said, slipping it into his billfold with my other school pictures.

In a few minutes, Dad went out to the barn.

As I stood in the porch a short while later putting on my chore coat and boots, I couldn't help thinking about Dad and what that must have been like. About walking in the deep snow. About seeing his dad fall down. About his dad dying right in front of him.

And all at once, as I pushed open the porch door and went out into the cold night air, I realized that my school pictures were not that important.

So what if my glasses made me look like a sick raccoon?

Who cared if I looked like I was peering out of a cave?

What difference did it make that I was not smiling?

It was only a picture, after all, and it wasn't like I would have to look at it everyday.

No, the truly important thing was Dad. He was alive and well and out in the barn milking right now and would soon have milk ready for me to carry to the milkhouse.

Although, by the time I got out to the barn, I decided I still would have been just as well satisfied if he had not insisted on keeping that dreadful picture in his billfold.

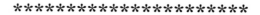

~ 7 ~
Thanksgiving Wishes

The thawed turkey sat on the counter in the big pan my sister used sometimes to bake oatmeal bars. The bar recipe made more batter than what would fit in a regular cake pan, so that's why she used the big pan. The turkey had been in the refrigerator for a couple of days, and since Thanksgiving was tomorrow, my sister had taken it out.

I had just come in from the barn after carrying milk and feeding the calves. As I pulled out a chair and sat down by the table, my mother reached into the cupboard for the box of salt. "Morton Salt" it said in white letters on the dark blue label. It also said, "when it rains, it pours," and there was a picture of a little girl carrying an umbrella.

"What does that mean?" I said. "'When it rains, it pours.'"

"What?" my mother asked.

"On the box of salt. 'When it rains, it pours.'"

"Oh, that," she said. "They put something into the salt so it won't draw moisture out of the air and form hard chunks."

"Chunks?" I said.

My sister stood by the stove, stirring a pan of cranberries as they cooked.

"You know how the sugar gets in the summer when it's humid. All full of hard lumps. The salt would do the same thing, except then you wouldn't be able to get it out of the box," Loretta explained.

"Why wouldn't you be able to get it out of the box?" I asked.

"The spout is too small," Mom said.

My sister reached over and turned the burner dial down to a lower setting. Then she went back to stirring the cranberries, which made the kitchen smell like summer when Mom made jam or jelly, sweet and tangy, all at the same time.

During supper, Loretta had said she wanted to make the cranberry sauce tonight so it could chill in the refrigerator. She had found a new recipe in a magazine. When the cranberry sauce had finished cooking, she was going to put it into a round gelatin mold.

Holding onto the cupboard with her left hand, my mother used her right hand to open the salt box. She poured some inside the turkey and set the box on the counter. My stomach performed a small flip-flop as she put her hand inside the turkey.

"How can you do that?" I asked.

"Do what?" Mom said.

"Who?" Loretta said.

"Mom," I said. "How can you put your hand inside the turkey like that?"

My mother paused and shrugged. "How else am I going to rub the salt in?"

I did not know if there was another way to rub salt on the inside of the turkey, but I was glad it wasn't me. I couldn't help feeling sorry for the poor turkey, although by tomorrow, when the turkey came out of the oven golden brown, I knew I would forget all about feeling sorry.

My mother finished rubbing in the salt. She poured more salt on the outside of the turkey.

"I have to confess," Mom said as she went to work rubbing in the salt, "that I don't really feel much like Thanksgiving this year."

"Why not?" I asked.

My mother used her forearm to push a lock of her curly dark hair back from her forehead.

"It's not Thanksgiving so much, I guess," she said. "But what I'd like to know is—how is a person supposed to get in the mood for Christmas? We don't even have any snow on the ground yet."

I swallowed hard and crossed my fingers.

"Christmas?" I said cautiously.

From past experience, I knew that if anybody so much as mentioned the word "Christmas" before Thanksgiving was over, Mom practically exploded. She said she wanted to get one holiday out of the way before she started thinking about the next one. I made the mistake a few years ago of saying that Dad and I should cut a Christmas tree before Thanksgiving in case there was too much snow to get out in the field after Thanksgiving. My mother wouldn't even let us talk about it. So we waited. By the time we did go out, there was so much snow, the pickup truck got stuck.

"That's what I said. Christmas," my mother replied as she continued rubbing salt into the turkey. "I just cannot get in the mood for Christmas when there's no snow."

"But," I said, "I thought you didn't like snow."

"Snow is fine in December because it's not Christmas without snow," she said. "But after that. Well, after that, it's a different story if we get a lot of snow. And usually we do."

I knew what she was talking about. Dad made sure he shoveled the path out to the driveway wide enough so Mom could get through with her crutches. But sometimes in February and especially in March, the path turned icy, and then Mom was stuck in the house until the ice melted. Dad said he could put down some salt to melt the ice, but Mom said she did not want the salt to kill the grass. She also said she did not want people to drag salt in the house on their feet. The sand we dragged in the rest of the year was bad enough, she said.

My mother gave the turkey one final rub and then slid her feet sideways, first one and then the other, hanging onto the counter with one hand until she reached the sink. She turned on the water, leaned against the counter on both forearms and washed the salt off her hands.

"I know it hasn't been very warm lately," Mom said while she dried her hands. "But in the past few weeks, since it stopped raining so much and it's been sunny, I haven't even wanted to *think* about Christmas, much less think about buying Christmas presents."

My sister stopped stirring the cranberries, turned off the burner, and went back to stirring. "You know," she said. "Now that you mention it, I haven't thought much about Christmas, either."

I looked back and forth between Mom and Loretta.

I could hardly believe my ears.

"You haven't thought about Christmas at all?" I said in a dry, squeaky little voice.

"Nope," Mom said.

"Not really," Loretta said.

A little while later I went upstairs to put my pajamas on. Enough light filtered up from the kitchen so I could see to turn on the lamp beside my bed. The single bulb overhead turned on and off with a pull chain, except that I was not tall enough to reach it and would have to stand on a chair.

After I put my pajamas on—white flannel pants and a top with little pink flowers—I crawled under the covers and picked up the book I had been reading. I always read at least a few pages before I went to sleep. The book was about a girl from the city who went to visit her cousins who lived on a ranch out West. She was learning how to ride a horse. I had read the book before, but I liked it so much, I wanted to read it again.

By the time I found myself reading the same page over for the third time, I decided to give up and reached over to turn off the lamp. I pulled the covers up to my chin and laid there with my eyes wide open.

Was it really true that Mom had not thought about Christmas yet? And what if we didn't get any snow at all this winter? I knew that would never happen because it always snowed, although sometimes we did not get much snow until after Christmas.

But if it didn't snow soon, did that mean we would not have any Christmas presents? Or cookies? Or a Christmas tree?

Or maybe not even any lefse?

My mother baked lefse a couple of times during December. If Thanksgiving came a week early, then sometimes she baked lefse in November, too. Christmas was the only time my mother baked the flat Norwegian pastry made out of potatoes and flour and butter and milk.

I would happily eat nothing but lefse for breakfast, dinner and supper, if Mom would let me. There was something about a piece of lefse spread with butter and sprinkled with sugar and cinnamon that made my mouth water just thinking about it.

But now, because we didn't have any snow, we might not have Christmas.

And Mom probably would not bake lefse.

After what seemed like a very long time, I finally began to feel sleepy. My last thought, before I drifted off to sleep was, '*I wish we would get a really big snowstorm. I wish we would get a really big snowstorm...*'

As soon as I woke up the next morning, I leaped out of bed and hurried over to the window that faced toward the barn.

It was just as I had feared. The ground was still brown. Not a snowflake in sight.

I got dressed and went down the steps into the kitchen. Mom had already put the turkey into the oven.

"It didn't snow last night," I said.

"No, of course not," Mom replied. "The weather forecast said it's supposed to be sunny today. Cold. But sunny."

I went out into the porch to put on my chore coat and boots. Ingman was scheduled on the three-to-eleven shift at the creamery this week and had already gone out to the barn to help Dad milk. But as I walked toward the barn across the bare ground with no snow, the thought that Ingman would be home for Thanksgiving dinner made me feel only a little better. What good was Thanksgiving dinner if there wasn't going to be any Christmas?

Early that afternoon, we sat down to eat dinner. I barely noticed Loretta's special cranberry sauce or the candied sweet potatoes. The sun was still shining, although it seemed to me, as I helped myself to more turkey, that maybe the sun wasn't quite as bright as it had been in the morning.

For several years, I had been in the habit of reading a couple of Christmas books after we had finished eating Thanksgiving dinner. I was really too old for the books. They were children's books. I had gotten them as Christmas presents when I was a very little girl. Mom had read them to me at first when I did not know how to read myself. One was called *Rudolph the Red-Nosed Reindeer,* and the other was called *The Christmas Story* and was about Mary and Joseph and Baby Jesus.

Today, I did not feel like reading them at all.

By the time I went out to the barn with Dad to feed the cows, the sun had started to set. A few clouds had gathered on the horizon, but otherwise, the sky was clear.

"When is it going to snow, Daddy?" I asked as we walked across the yard.

I zipped my coat all the way up and then pulled my stocking cap down over my ears. Now that the sun was almost gone, the air definitely felt cold.

Dad shrugged. "The radio said this morning that we might get flurries tonight."

Flurries. Only a few snowflakes to make the air look pretty for a while. But nothing more than that.

I drew a deep breath and let it slowly.

"Something bothering you, kiddo?" Dad asked.

"Mom said that without any snow, she's not in the mood for Christmas," I said.

I walked into the barn behind Dad and then pulled the door shut.

"Daddy, she hasn't even *thought* about Christmas."

My father smiled. "Don't get too upset just yet. The weather can change in an awful hurry this time of year."

I knew Dad was right. But still—what if we did not get any snow until January?

That night, once again I fell asleep thinking, *"I wish we would get a really big snowstorm. I wish we would get a really big snowstorm..."*

The next morning, as soon as I woke up, I threw back the covers and rushed over to the window.

The ground was as bare and brown as it had been yesterday.

On the Friday after Thanksgiving, Loretta and Mom always went Christmas shopping. Loretta said it was the first official day of the Christmas season. She also said it was fun to see how the different stores were decorated, almost as if by magic, because on Wednesday, none of them had put up a single Christmas decoration.

I had to take my sister's word for it that the stores would be decorated for Christmas today. I was not allowed to go with Mom and Loretta the day after Thanksgiving.

While we were eating breakfast, my big sister asked about going shopping, but Mom shook her head.

"Nope, I'm not in the mood. You can go, though, if you want to."

Loretta shrugged. "No, that's all right. It's not much fun to go by myself."

I could barely swallow my bite of pancakes. For the first time that I could remember, Mom and Loretta were not going shopping the day after Thanksgiving.

Later on in the morning, I headed out to Dusty's pasture to check on her water. If the ice was not too thick, she would break it with her nose or lick at it until she had made a spot where she could drink. During the week when I was in school, Dad would check Dusty's water and would thaw out her bucket and bring warm water for her. On the weekends, I checked Dusty's water myself. The milkhouse had a water heater and plenty of hot water.

Our dog, Needles, came out of the granary to meet me, his cream-colored tail going in circles. Lately he had been spending quite a lot of time in the granary, curled up on the burlap feed sacks Dad put down for him.

Dad said he was worried because the dog refused to stay in the barn at night. One time when we were ready to go to the house, Dad had told Needles "stay" and had shut the barn door. But as soon as we started to walk away, the dog began yipping and barking and howling. Dad let him out then. He said it would make the cows too nervous if Needles kept that up for very long. "I wish you'd stay in the barn where it's warm," Dad had said.

Needles acted like he could not get out of the barn fast enough. He had pranced beside us as we walked to the house, and when we reached the steps, he had turned and headed for the granary. Since earlier in the fall, Dad had made sure the door was propped open enough so Needles could go in and out as he pleased. "It's not so bad now, but I don't know what we're going to do with Needles this winter when it's below zero," Dad had said as he watched the dog trotting toward the granary.

Needles and I made our way to the spot behind the corncrib where I had tied Dusty's water bucket to a fence post. Early on, I had learned that it was a good idea to tie Dusty's water bucket. She loved to play with the bucket and would tip it over any chance she got.

The moment I untied the twine string so I could pick up the bucket, a tiny wet speck landed on my cheek.

"What was that?" I said.

Dusty had come over to the fence, and Needles had sat down next to me. He was not too sure about going into Dusty's pasture by himself. Sometimes the pony chased him and would try to bite his tail. Dad said it was because she was mischievous and wanted to play. He said if Dusty truly did not like Needles, she would try to strike him with her front feet.

Needles looked up at me. One round brown eye twitched open-and-shut, open-and-shut, as if he were winking at me. Then I realized he had two white specks on his eyelashes.

They were snowflakes.

I looked at Dusty. Her dapples had disappeared when her winter hair started to grow, and now she was solid brown. The pony had snowflakes scattered on her back, clinging to the fuzzy brown hair.

Dusty's winter coat was so thick that it almost covered my hand when I pushed my fingers into her hair.

"It's snowing!" I said. "It's snowing!"

Dusty's water bucket had frozen over and was only one-third full, so I knew I would have to thaw it out and bring warm water for her. As I pulled the bucket under the fence, the snowflakes began to fall a little faster.

Needles followed me to the milkhouse and sat in the corner to watch while I ran hot water into Dusty's bucket and swirled it around to melt the ice. I put hot water in the bucket and then cold until the water felt pleasantly warm to my fingers. When Needles and I came out of the milkhouse a while later, the snowflakes were falling harder yet.

I tied the bucket to the fence for Dusty and then raced for the house, with Needles right behind me, barking.

"It's snowing!" I said as I burst into the kitchen. "It's snowing."

"Yes," Mom said. "I can see that."

My mother stood by the kitchen sink, looking out the west window. The snow was falling fast enough now that the dark green pines at the back of the twenty-acre field behind the barn were blurry, as if someone had hung Mom's white chiffon curtains in front of them. The kitchen curtains had ruffles and were almost as long as the tall kitchen windows. On each side, they were gathered back with a ruffled tie.

When Dad and Ingman came in the house for dinner, it was snowing so hard that I could barely see the pines at the back of the farm.

"I thought the weather forecast said a few flurries," Mom said.

"It did. That's what they said on the radio," Dad said as he hung his blue-and-white pin-striped chore cap on the newel post at the bottom of the steps.

A little while later, after Dad and Ingman had washed their hands, we sat down to eat turkey and gravy and biscuits. Loretta had baked biscuits and had cut up more of the leftover turkey. From what I could see, we were going to have to eat a couple more meals of turkey before Mom could pick the rest of the meat off the twenty-pound bird to make soup.

"Would you say the table prayer, please," Mom asked, looking over at me.

I folded my hands and bowed my head. "By thy goodness, all are fed. We thank the Lord for daily bread. Amen."

"Amen," my mother said. She turned to look at the kitchen window where snowflakes swirled against the glass.

"I'm glad we made extra mashed potatoes for Thanksgiving dinner," Mom said as she turned back to the table.

"Why's that?" Dad asked.

"Christmas isn't all that far off, you know," she said. "I think I'll bake some lefse this afternoon."

By the next morning, we had nearly a foot of fluffy, white, new snow.

"I should have known better," Mom muttered as she gazed out the window. "Here I am always reminding people they have to be careful what they wish for. When I said I wished we had some snow to make it feel more like Christmas, I did not mean a foot."

Well. Maybe my mother had not wished for a foot of snow.

But as I slathered a piece of lefse with butter, I was sure glad I did.

****

8

A Shelter From the Storm

Two weeks after a foot of snow had fallen during Thanksgiving vacation, Mom, Dad and I went to the farm supply store on Saturday afternoon. I needed new chore boots because my old ones were getting too small. Dad needed grease, links for the manure spreader chains and a few nuts and bolts "just in case." Mom came along for the ride but stayed in the car. She and Loretta had gone Christmas shopping the previous Saturday.

While we were in town, it started to snow.

By the time we arrived home, it was still snowing in a thick curtain of big, wet, heavy flakes.

"Oh, no," my mother muttered as we rounded the curve at the top of our driveway. "Don't tell me we're going to go through this again."

"Go through what again?" Dad asked.

"Look at Dusty," Mom replied.

From the driveway, we could see Dusty, my little brown pony with the white mane and tail, standing with her head inside the chicken coop door. You could not really tell that she was brown, though, because at the moment, Dusty was covered with a layer of snow.

"Why does she do that?" Mom asked as Dad turned the car toward the house. "Why doesn't she go inside?"

Since we did not have chickens anymore, Dad had figured that the chicken coop would make a good shelter for my pony. We had gotten rid of the chickens a few years earlier. Mom said she would rather not have chicken manure scattered around the yard. Dad said that because of where the barnyard was located, there was no room to build a chicken yard to keep them around the chicken coop. Mom said we could always buy eggs from the neighbors. One neighbor girl raised chickens for her 4-H project and always had eggs to sell.

The chicken coop stood inside Dusty's pasture. It still smelled like chickens, but the coop was a snug little building that could keep the wind and snow off my pony.

There was only one problem.

Dusty refused to go inside.

All last winter, when it was snowing, or when it was cold and windy, Dusty would stand with her head inside the chicken coop door. Dad and I had tried to lead the pony into the chicken coop countless times to show her that she could go in and out as she pleased. We would get right up to the door, but then Dusty would refuse to take another step.

At other times, we would think we were making progress when Dusty would walk right in. But as soon as Dad or I let go of her halter, she would turn around and go back outside again.

Dad said he had no idea why Dusty would not stay in the chicken coop.

"I spent an awful lot of years around workhorses, and from what I can see, she's a very smart little pony," he said. "She ought to know that going inside is a good idea when the weather is bad."

After a while, I asked Dad if we could put Dusty in the barn. He agreed. "It's not good for an animal to stand outside in a wind chill, especially when it's below zero," he said.

My mother would not hear of it.

"Cows belong in the barn. Dusty's got the chicken coop," she said. "When the weather gets bad enough, she will go inside."

Mom had not been especially crazy about the idea of me getting a pony in the first place, so of course I should have known that she would not want Dusty to stay in the barn.

And right now, as the snow fell in wet, heavy, thick flakes, it looked as if my pony was going to spend another winter standing with her head inside the chicken coop.

As Dad brought the car to a halt, my mother heaved a deep sigh. Mom had worn a blue checkered wool scarf over her head on the way out to the car, but once the car had started to warm up, she had put the scarf around her neck. She looked at Dad and then at me as she fingered the fringe around the edge of the scarf.

"Well," she said, "I guess that does it then."

"What does what?" Dad asked.

"I simply cannot stand it anymore," Mom said.

"Stand what?" Dad asked.

"She's just doing that on purpose," my mother muttered.

"What are you talking about?" Dad inquired. He reached up and nudged his cap aside so he could scratch the top of his ear. Dad kept a new cap to wear to town, the same kind of pin-striped cap he wore all summer long even though it was cold out now. When he worked outside in the winter, then he wore a wool cap with flaps that he could pull down over his ears.

"That pony," my mother said. "I just know she's doing it on purpose. I can't take another winter of seeing her covered with snow every time we get a blizzard."

Dad shrugged. "I don't know how many times we tried to show her that she can go in the chicken coop."

My mother heaved another sigh. "That's what I mean … if she's not going to take advantage of the chicken coop … well … I think you should put her in the barn."

I took off my stocking cap. Maybe the knitted material was blocking my hearing because what I thought I heard from my position in the back seat was—I *thought* Mom had said we should put Dusty in the barn.

"What did you say?" I asked.

"I said, maybe you should put Dusty in the barn," my mother replied.

"In the barn?" I said.

"Yes, in the barn," Mom said.

"Well…" Dad said, throwing a brief wink in my direction, "I guess it's not so bad on a day like today when it's just snowing, but when we've got a wind chill…"

"I should've told you to put her in the barn last year," my mother said. "Could have saved myself a lot of worry."

"You were worried?" I said. "About Dusty?"

"Yes, I was worried about Dusty."

"I thought you didn't like Dusty."

"Of course I like Dusty. I don't like horses," Mom said, "but Dusty is different. I don't want her to be cold. And I certainly wouldn't want her to get sick."

During the long years I had spent trying to convince my mother to let me get a pony, Mom always said she did not like horses. She used to have to drive the workhorses for the hay fork to put hay up in the haymow, and she said she was always afraid of "those great big things."

While we were sitting in the car talking, the snow had continued to fall. In only a few minutes, the windshield was already covered in white. My mother opened her car door.

"Come inside and change your clothes," she said to me. "And then you can help Dad bring Dusty in the barn."

"Are you sure, Ma?" Dad asked.

"I'm sure. I can't stand worrying about her anymore."

It seemed that I spent a great deal of time during the day changing from one kind of clothes to another. I had one set of clothes for being in the house, another set for going out to the barn to help with the chores, and a third set for going somewhere—school, church, town. Sometimes the "being at home" clothes and the "chore" clothes were the same.

During the winter, when I wore a coat out in the barn, I would just change my pants before helping with the chores. Then I would change out of my chore pants when I came back in the house. Mom said the house already smelled enough like the barn without me wearing a pair of pants that smelled like the barn, too.

My father also changed his clothes before we went out to the barn to put Dusty inside. He liked to wear clean clothes when he went into a store. I could always tell if someone had come straight from the barn when we went to town and stopped at the grocery store or the bank or the restaurant. The powerful smell of cow manure hung around that person in an eye-watering cloud. It was kind of a funny thing, too, because whenever I was out in the barn at home, I never noticed the smell.

A little while later, Dad and I headed out to the barn. When we came around the corner of the garage, I looked over and saw Needles coming down the granary steps. The dog stopped, shook himself and then stretched, taking a bow with his front end before he worked the kinks out of his hind legs. As he came toward us, he stopped once to shake the snow out of his fur.

"How are ya, pup?" Dad said, reaching down to pat Needles on the head. The dog wagged his tail faster.

"Now, let's see," Dad said, as reached for the latch on the barn door. "We don't have any calves in the pen on this end, so maybe we should put Dusty in there."

I followed Dad into the barn, with Needles right on my heels.

"This end of the barn will be better," Dad continued, "because then it will be easier to take her outside to her pasture during the day."

"Why can't Dusty stay inside all day?" I asked. "The calves stay inside."

Dad shook his head. "With all that thick hair, I think Dusty would get too warm. Plus, she needs to get outside for some exercise."

I hadn't thought of that.

The calf pen where Dad said we should put Dusty occupied the corner on the east end of the barn next to the milkhouse. Thumper's cage was on top of the calf pen wall in the corner by the door, which made it easy for me to clean the white rabbit's cage with the "cage cleaner" Dad had made from an old broom handle and an old blade from a sickle mower. I used the scraper to pull out the soiled bedding and then swept it into the gutter with the push broom.

Two more calf pens were situated on either side of the aisle on the other end of the barn. We had a couple of little calves only a few weeks old. By the time summer came and the calves were too big to stay in the pens all the time, they would go outside when the cows went outside and would come in to eat their feed when the cows came in.

"Before we get Dusty, we'll have to spread some straw out for her," Dad said. He headed for the haymow ladder. One corner of the mow was full of straw that we had baled after Dad had harvested oats.

"I think we'll need two bales," Dad said as I followed behind him.

"I'll throw down a bale, and then you can carry it to the pen and start spreading it out. I'll bring the other bale," my father said.

The cows were still outside. Dad had let them out just before he came in the house for dinner. He said it would be good for them to get some fresh air and to move around for a while.

The cows must have known we were in the barn because I could hear them just outside the door at the other end. Occasionally one of them said *mooooooo* low in her throat, as if she were wondering when someone was going to open the door. After we had spread out bedding in Dusty's stall and had brought her inside, it would be time to put cow feed in the mangers and to let the cows in.

I could hear Dad walking toward the hay hole across the ceiling above my head, so I moved back a few steps.

"Are you out of the way?" Dad yelled.

"Yes!" I said.

"Okay, here it comes."

With a *whoosh* and a *thump*, the straw bale landed on the floor. When I was a very little girl, Dad had taught me it was important not to stand under the hay hole when someone was throwing down hay or straw. "The bales are not all that heavy, but when they're coming down from the mow, they could knock you down and hurt you," he'd said.

Sometimes when Dad or Ingman threw down hay or straw, one of the barn cats would sit underneath the hay hole, looking up toward the ceiling. I was amazed at how fast the barn cats could move. As soon as they heard the *whoosh* of a bale coming down, they high-tailed it out of there. Before the bale landed with a *thump*, the cat was safely somewhere else. I thought it seemed like a game they played, to see how fast they could get out of the way.

Needles knew enough to stay out of the way, too. Since the cows were not in the barn, he had curled up in the straw in the first stall by the feed box, nose in his tail.

I stepped forward and grabbed the two twine strings that went around the bale of straw, one in each hand. Straw was easy to carry seeing as it did not weigh very much.

I carried the straw down to the end of the row of stanchions, turned and went across the gutter. As I passed by Needles, he lifted his head, looked at me with sleepy eyes, and put his nose back into his tail.

After I set the bale down in the calf pen, I pulled the twine off and began scattering straw.

"We want it pretty thick," Dad said, bringing the second bale into the pen, "so Dusty's feet won't get sore from standing on the concrete.

Dad reached for his pocket knife to cut open the bale. "Cows can't stand on concrete too well, either, but they can stand on it better than horses."

Together we shook out the rest of the straw. The smell reminded me of the oatmeal Dad cooked for breakfast sometimes. It also made me think of the warm summer days in August when my father brought the combine out of the shed and went to work combining oats.

"Okay, that should do it," Dad said. He wound the twine strings into a loop and put them in the barrel near the door. Half a bale of hay sat in the corner by the feed box. He put a flake into the calf pen manger.

"Now—let's go get your pony," he said, heading for the door.

The snow was falling as thickly as it had been when we got home from town. As I knew he would, Needles was awake the moment Dad touched the latch on the barn door. He jumped to his feet and followed us outside. Dusty was still standing with her head in the chicken coop.

"How much is it going to snow, Daddy?" I asked as we walked past the milk house.

"I have no idea," Dad said. "So far I'd say we've got about four inches. If it keeps up like this all night, we'll have two feet."

With Needles still beside us, we made our way past the corn crib.

"Hey, Dusty, wadda ya think?" Dad asked.

My pony backed up hastily and turned her head toward us.

"Weren't expecting us, were you," Dad said.

"Daddy, what about a lead rope and a halter. We forgot a lead rope and a halter."

"Don't need 'em," Dad said as he climbed through the fence.

"Why not?"

"You'll see."

My father grabbed hold of the pony's thick white forelock and started walking toward the gate. Dusty hesitated once and then followed along beside him. As she moved, snow slid off her flanks.

"I didn't know you could lead horses that way!" I said.

"This is how we used to lead the workhorses," Dad said.

I took Dusty's halter off when I put her back in the pasture. If I left the halter on, then in a day or two, I would have to walk back and forth through the grass until I found it. Dusty was very good at slipping the halter off. Dad said it was because she liked to scratch her ears on anything that did not move.

When we reached the gate, I opened it for Dad and Dusty. The top and bottom of the gatepost fit into wire loops to keep the gate closed. I pulled the gate back and then propped the post against the fence.

With his hand still grasping her forelock, Dad led Dusty toward the barn. Needles trotted along next to Dad.

"I hope you like the calf pen, Dusty," Dad said.

"Why wouldn't she like the calf pen?" I asked.

"Maybe that's why she won't go in the chicken coop, because she doesn't like being inside of a building," Dad said.

I thought about this for a bit.

"But Daddy. I bring Dusty inside the barn sometimes when I brush her."

"Oh, I know she's been inside," Dad said. "But there's a difference between coming inside for a visit and staying inside. She might not like staying inside."

Oh, sure, my father would have to think of something like that.

Dusty quietly walked into the barn next to Dad and then into the calf pen, as if she had been doing it every day of her life.

My father let go of the pony's foretop. She immediately went to the manger to see what might be in there and found the flake of hay Dad had put in the corner.

Thumper sat up on his haunches to stare at Dusty. His pink nose wiggled as he lifted his head to sniff the air.

Dad laughed. "You've got company now, Thumper."

The pony grabbed a mouthful of hay, and then, with hay sticking out both sides of her mouth, chewed and looked around the barn, her brown eyes bright with curiosity.

"Let's see what she does if we leave the barn," Dad said. "She might be all right if we're standing here but not okay if we leave."

We went outside and closed the barn door. Dad leaned forward, his ear next to the latch.

"Hear anything?" I asked.

Dad shook his head.

We waited a few minutes, the snow still falling in a thick curtain. After a while, Dad shrugged and reached for the door latch.

"If Dusty was going to raise a ruckus, she'd have done it by now, I think," he said.

As soon as I got in the barn, I could see Dusty still calmly chewing her hay. Dad and I stopped to brush the snow off our coats. The pony turned her head toward us, finished her mouthful of hay and reached for another, tearing it out of the manger with a sharp tug.

"Did you see that?" Dad asked. "When they eat hay like that, they're happy."

I had seen cows grab mouthfuls of hay just like that. You could almost see them smiling, as if they were feeling both playful and hungry.

Dad turned and walked toward the feed box. "Now that we've got Dusty settled in, we'd better put the cows in. They're going to be all wet with snow as it is."

"Daddy," I said, as I picked up the bucket of feed Dad had filled. "You don't think Dusty will be afraid of the cows coming in the barn, do you?"

My father shook his head as he filled another bucket. "Nope. Why would she be afraid of the cows? She sees them all the time from her pasture."

I carried buckets of feed to one side of the barn and poured out feed in front of each stanchion, and Dad carried feed to the other side. When we were finished, my father went to the other end of the barn and opened the door. The cows rushed in, one by one. Snow slid off their backs, landing on the floor with a soft *plop* as they hurried toward their stanchions.

Dad pursed his lips and sighed. "At least it'll be just the floor that's wet and not their straw."

When the cows started coming in the barn, Needles sat down by the twine barrel. He knew he was out of way there and safe from the ones who liked to chase him.

In between mouthfuls of hay, Dusty watched the cows.

After all of the cows had come in, while Dad shut the stanchions on one side of the barn, I shut the stanchions on the other. One cow was down on her knees. She had figured out that if she dropped to her knees, she could reach farther and would be able to help her neighbors eat their feed, too. Dad called her Chubby. Cows were funny that way. Some ate their feed fast, like Chubby, and looked for more, while others ate more slowly and were content with their own pile of feed.

"Daddy, should I give Dusty a pail of water?" I said when we had finished shutting the stanchions.

"Fill a calf pail and put it in the manger," Dad said. "She might learn how to drink from the water cup after a while, but for now, we can give her a pail."

The calf pen manger had its own water cup. To me, the water cups looked like upside down army helmets. Each cup had a paddle in the middle that the cows pushed down with their noses to fill the cup so they could drink.

When I had given Dusty a pail of water and we had fed the cows hay, Dad and I were ready to go to the house for supper. Thumper had gotten over his curiosity about Dusty and was now sound asleep.

"Leaving or staying?" Dad asked, looking down at Needles.

The dog came closer to the door and wagged his tail.

"Leaving, it looks like," my father said, "which I should have known already without asking."

Outside, it was still snowing, although the flakes were smaller now.

Needles trotted beside us to the house steps and then turned and trotted off toward the granary.

When Dad opened the kitchen door, Mom was waiting.

"Well?" she said.

"Well, what?" Dad asked.

"Well? How did it go with Dusty?"

"Like I thought it would," Dad said. "She walked right in and made herself to home."

"Oh, good," Mom said. "Now I don't have to worry about her."

Dad hung his chore cap on the newel post. "I thought maybe she wouldn't go into the chicken coop because she didn't want to be inside of a building. But that's not it. She walked right into the calf pen and started eating hay."

"Dusty was outside at the pony farm, in a pasture, wasn't she?" Mom asked.

"I think she's always been outside. I don't think they ever kept her in the barn," Dad replied.

"Well," Mom said, "I wouldn't put it past her not to go in the chicken coop because she knew I'd let you put her in the barn. I think she did it on purpose."

I could see Dad was trying not to smile.

"She's a smart little pony, Ma. But I don't think she's that smart. She'd have to be a mind reader on top of everything else."

For a long time after that, whenever we put Dusty in the barn because it was snowing or cold and windy, I thought about what Mom had said. Dusty loved being in the barn. She would nicker, like she was chuckling with glee, when Dad or I gave her a big handful of cow feed while we were feeding the cows. Dad said Dusty should not eat too much of the ground corn and oats mixed with molasses because it might make her sick, although a little bit was all right.

Of course, Dusty did not always nicker when Dad or I came with a bucket of feed.

Sometimes she whinnied.

The only other time I had heard her whinny like that was the night we had brought her home in the back of our old pickup truck. As we drove along, she would let out a long, loud whinny now and again. Dad said she was talking to the cows out in the pasture along the way, telling them, "Look at meeeee! I'm going hoooooome!"

Was it possible that Dusty never went in the chicken coop because she would rather be in the barn?

Naaaaa…couldn't be…

9

Snowbound

I had not even set my books on the table yet when my mother asked the question she always asked when I came home—"What did you do in school today?" Most of the time, it was hard for me to think of an answer because usually it did not seem like we had done much of anything.

But today was different.

"We started reading a poem in English class," I said as I went to the hall closet to hang up my coat.

"A long one or a short one?" Mom asked.

My mother was sitting by the table with a piece of cake and a cup of coffee. If my mother had baked a cake in the afternoon, she would cut a piece for herself and one for me about the time she knew I would be coming home from school.

"It's a long one," I said as I sat down at the table by my piece of cake. Today Mom had baked a chocolate cake with white frosting.

I actually had no way of knowing if the poem was short or long. I had very little experience with poems, except for the few we had read in English. The poem seemed long to me, though, because it took up quite a few pages in the book.

"What's the poem about?" my mother asked.

The poem, in fact, covered a subject near and dear to my heart. Or at least the subject was near and dear to my heart during the winter.

"It's about a snowstorm," I said. "A really big, huge snowstorm that turns into a blizzard."

"Let's see…," my mother replied, "a snowstorm that turns into a blizzard. Does it start out talking about how the sun gradually becomes covered with clouds and the way the sky looks, and that's how they know it's going to snow and that there's going to be a blizzard?"

I quickly finished chewing my bite of cake. Mom said it was impolite to talk with food in your mouth.

"How did you know? About the sun? And the way the poem started out?" I asked.

"Is it the one called 'Snowbound' by John Greenleaf Whittier?" Mom replied.

I forgot all about eating my cake. "How did you know *that*?"

My mother smiled. "We read it when I was in school, too."

"You did?"

"And we made a booklet. I've still got it yet. As I recall, the cover was blue. I think it was blue, anyway."

"Where's the booklet?" I asked.

Our teacher said we would have to make a booklet, too, so if Mom still had her booklet, I was curious to see what it looked like.

"Yes, I've still got the booklet," Mom said. "It's in the cedar chest."

The little cedar chest was upstairs. I had never seen any other cedar chest, but Mom said it was a little one. Big cedar chests were made to hold blankets and quilts and clothing that people did not want the moths to chew up, she said. The little cedar chest measured maybe three feet by two feet and had been made for her by her Uncle John for her birthday when she was ten years old.

Mom's Uncle John had died a long time before I was born. He was Norwegian and a carpenter and he had only one arm. He had lost the other arm in an accident, although having one arm had not stopped him from being a carpenter. Mom's little cedar chest was made of both red and white cedar. She kept important things in it: pictures and wedding invitations and birth certificates and baptismal certificates— and now, as I had found out—school booklets.

I suppose I should not have been surprised my mother would keep a booklet she had made when she went to the little one-room country school a mile from our farm. I was the only one of four children who had been born in the hospital. If my mother had also kept the plastic bracelet they put around my ankle that said "Girl Ralph" on it, why wouldn't she keep a booklet she had made in school?

"I wish we would get a snowstorm like that," I said.

The more days we could get off from school, the better I liked it.

Oh, sure, sometimes we got enough snow so that school was closed for a day, but we had never gotten enough snow so the roads were closed for days on end like they were in the poem. I could not imagine what it would be like for our farm to be closed off from the rest of the world. The milk truck had a plow blade on the front. How much snow would have to fall before there would be too much snow for the milk truck driver to clear the driveway on his way to the milkhouse to pick up our milk?

"We used to get snowstorms like that," Mom said, using her fork to cut another bite of cake.

I knew my mother had walked to school when she was a kid. Sometimes, however, if there was quite a bit of snow or it was cold and windy, I also knew her dad had hooked up the team of horses to give her a ride to school.

"Did you have to go to school when you got a big snowstorm?" I asked when I had finished chewing another bite of cake.

Mom set her coffee cup down on the table. My mother said all "good Norwegians" loved to drink coffee.

"Yes, we had to go to school when there was a big snowstorm. Usually anyway. Sometimes if it was snowing too hard to see where I was going I'd stay home. I've already told you about my dad hooking up the team to take me if there was a lot of snow or if it was cold and windy."

To my way of thinking, my mother was really lucky. It would be so much fun to have horses and cutters and sleds. After Mom had said she used to get rides to school, I had told her she was lucky, and she had looked at me and said, "The 'good old days' were not as 'good' as some people might like to think." I was not exactly sure what she meant by that. What could be better than riding to school behind a team of horses?

"After we got a big snowstorm," Mom continued, "if there was too much snow for the horses to get through, then I would put on my skis."

I paused with my fork poised in mid air.

"You put on what?"

"Skis."

"Skis?"

"Yes. Cross-country skis."

"You mean the kind of skis that people use in the snow?" I said.

"Yes," she said.

I knew people used skis to go down long hills. But I had never heard of cross-country skis.

"What are cross-country skis?" I asked.

"Just what they sound like. Instead of going down hill, you ski across the countryside. It's sort of like skating, except you have skis on your feet, and you use poles to help push yourself along. The ones I had were shorter and wider, though, than the ones I've seen in magazines," she explained.

I had a hard time picturing my mother using cross-country skis. Because of the polio paralysis, getting around the house was not so easy for her, never mind getting around outside when there was snow on the ground.

"I know what you're thinking," Mom said.

"You do?"

"I wasn't always crippled, you know. And when I was a kid, I was pretty good on skis," she said.

I savored another small bite of cake. In my mind's eye, I could picture a little girl with a long, red scarf wound around her neck, and knitted mittens on her hands, gliding across the snow, headed for school. I don't know why the scarf should have been red. Maybe because it seemed to me that red was a pretty color outside when there was snow—like the cardinals we saw sometimes back by the pine trees when we went to cut a Christmas tree.

"Was it fun skiing to school?" I asked.

Every morning I rode the bus for almost an hour, and in the afternoon, I rode the bus for almost another hour. Riding the bus was better now that my best friend, Vicki, rode the bus, too. But still—skiing to school sounded like it would be a whole lot more fun than riding the bus. Sometimes the bus was crowded, and we would have to sit three to a seat.

My mother took another sip of coffee. "Well, yes, I guess it was sort of fun to ski to school. I didn't only use the skis when we had a snowstorm. The roads weren't plowed back then, so after we had too much snow to walk or to take the horses, I quite often used my skis. It was a lot faster to go across the field than it was to take the road."

"The roads weren't plowed then?" I asked.

"They didn't have to be plowed. If we needed something from the Norton store, we could walk or take the horses if there wasn't too much snow. Or I could use my skis. And church was only a half mile," Mom said.

Sometimes my sister and I went to the little country store just down the road from where from the one-room school had been to get soda pop or other snacks. The school building was there, but it was no longer used as a school.

"I wish I could ski to school," I said.

My mother smiled. "Do you realize how long it would take you to ski all the way into town? You'd have to leave for school at six o'clock in the morning."

"Six o'clock?"

"You don't really travel that much faster on skis than you do on foot. We used to walk to town all the time when I was a kid."

"You did?"

"Yes, we walked to town," Mom said.

"Why? How come you didn't use the workhorses and a wagon?"

"My mother did not like to drive the horses. Or maybe Pa would be using the team to do something else. So we walked."

I had walked to church a couple of times when the weather was nice for special Sunday school Christmas practices on Saturday. Like Mom said, it was only a half a mile. Walking to church took about twenty minutes or a half hour, depending on how fast I walked. But it was six miles into town.

"How long did it take you to walk into town?" I asked.

"Oh, a couple of hours, I guess. My mother was a fast walker. Sometimes I had trouble keeping up with her."

"Didn't you get tired?"

"Not really," Mom said. "We were all used to walking."

"So you think it would take a couple of hours to get into town on skis?" I asked.

"I know it would," Mom said. "If you skied to school, you wouldn't get home until almost six at night."

I stopped to think. If I left at six in the morning and did not arrive home until six at night, that would be an awfully long day. In fact, it would be...

"That would be twelve hours for school!" I said. "Two hours there, two hours back and the rest of the day in school!"

"Yes," Mom said. "It would be."

And here I thought that an hour bus ride in the morning and another hour in the afternoon was bad enough.

"Why don't you go upstairs to the cedar chest and see if you can find my 'Snowbound' booklet. After all these years, I'm curious to see what it looks like again," my mother said.

"We have to make a booklet, too," I said, as I carried my plate and fork to the sink.

"You do?" Mom said.

"And we have to do some other stuff."

"Like what?"

"We have pages and pages of questions to write out the answers to. And we have vocabulary to look up. And we have to make up crossword puzzles using parts of the poem as clues. Plus we have to make booklets," I said.

"I think you're going to be very busy before you're done with 'Snowbound,'" Mom said.

I was surprised to see that my mother had a sad and wistful expression in her blue eyes.

"Did you like school, Mom?" I asked.

"Very much. I would have liked to be a teacher," she said.

"You wanted to be a *teacher*?"

"Yes."

"Why didn't you get to be a teacher?" I asked.

My mother sighed. "You had to finish high school and then you had to go to what was called 'normal school' before you could be a teacher. But I couldn't go."

"Why not?"

"I think I've told you about this before. My mother and father would have had to pay someone room and board in town for me to stay with them so I could go to high school. Norton School only went to eighth grade. They couldn't afford to pay room and board. And they needed me to help with the farm work."

"Why couldn't you walk to school? You walked to town," I said.

"Walking to town once in a while was one thing, but walking every day? That would take too long. Especially in the winter when it was twenty degrees below zero," Mom said. "And skiing would have been a very long way when it was twenty below, too."

I hadn't thought about what it would be like to ski if it was twenty degrees below zero. When it was twenty below, my feet felt like icicles while I was out in the barn with Dad. How cold would my feet get after a couple of hours of skiing?

"Go upstairs now and find the Snowbound booklet," my mother said.

"Yes, Mom," I said.

Well, okay. So maybe skiing to school wouldn't be all that much fun. Not if it was below zero.

But as I went up the steps to find Mom's Snowbound booklet, I still thought a big, huge snowstorm would be tons of fun. Especially if the roads were closed for a couple of days so the bus could not get through.

After all, isn't that what snowstorms are for? To get you out of school for a while?

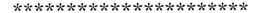

10

Hair Today... Gone Tomorrow

Every Friday evening after Loretta had moved to an apartment for the winter in the city where she worked, she would come home for the weekend. Usually my big sister arrived at five o'clock, and sometimes I was in the barn helping Dad feed the cows when she came home. If I was out in the barn, then I kept watching through the south windows, waiting for the headlights of her green Chevy Bel-Air to come over the first hill by the church.

Any headlights I saw would have to be Loretta's car. No one else lived along the road north of us. And our elderly next-door neighbors, Bill and Hannah Paulson, generally did not go anywhere in the evening.

On one particular Friday, when Loretta had not come home yet by 5:30, I knew something was out of the ordinary. So did Dad.

"Your sister must have gone shopping after work," Dad said. He leaned over to unroll the cuffs of his work overalls so he could brush out the hay chaff and the barn lime. Before Dad headed for the house, he always cleaned out his cuffs.

"Maybe she went Christmas shopping!" I said.

"Could be," Dad replied.

He straightened up. "Oh, nuts. I was going to see if I could fix that water cup before I went to the house, wasn't I."

Needles sat by Dad's feet, his tail slowly brushing back and forth across the white barn lime. My albino rabbit, Thumper, in his cage by Dusty's pen, nibbled a cob of corn that I had gone out the corn crib to get for him. Dusty stood with her head over the calf pen gate, watching us. The weather man on the radio in the barn said the temperature was not going to drop below zero, but a strong wind out of the north convinced Dad that Dusty should stay in the barn tonight.

"Which water cup do you have to fix?" I asked.

"The one by the ladder," Dad replied. "It isn't leaking much yet, but if it keeps up, the next thing you know, we'll come in the barn and find a manger full of water."

Sweeping water out of the concrete manger wasn't that much fun. If I was helping Dad feed the cows, it became my job to sweep out the water. Then, when we put out ground feed, it would stick where the manger was wet. The cows would not eat all of it, and then I had to sweep up sticky, wet cow feed. If we had already spread out hay in the manger when the water leak started and the hay got wet, the cows did not want to eat that, either.

Dad reached into the pliers pocket on the side of his work overalls.

"Maybe it's just stuck. Maybe I can fix it with this," he said, holding up the pliers.

Dad never went anywhere without the pliers he always carried in the little narrow pocket on his overalls made especially for that purpose.

My father headed up in front of the cows, with me right behind him. I would be able to see from the south window by the haymow ladder, so I could still keep an eye out for Loretta's headlights.

"Now—what's the matter here," Dad said.

A trickle of water flowed into the water cup, even though the cow was not drinking. At the moment, she was watching Dad, chewing a mouthful of hay.

My father lifted the paddle. Sometimes it did not spring all the way back when the cow finished drinking.

"Quit that," Dad muttered as he examined the paddle.

The cow next door had finished chewing her bite of hay and was now licking Dad's overalls.

"You're a pest. Do you know that?" he asked, as he rubbed the cow's forehead.

"Patches isn't a pest, Daddy!" I said.

Dad shook his head. "No, Patches isn't a pest. She's a *pet*." He grinned and went back to looking at the water cup paddle.

Patches stopped licking his overalls and started licking his elbow.

"What do you want me to do to help, Daddy?"

"You can pet Patches. Maybe she will leave me alone," Dad replied.

I moved over a few steps. I couldn't see out the window quite as well from here, but I could still see out the window.

"Patches," I said, "you're bothering Dad."

The black and white cow looked at me with her dark eyes, and then her tongue, rough as sandpaper, darted out and she started to lick my chore pants—*scritch, scritch, scritch.*

"Oh," Dad said. "So this is the problem." He held up what looked like a thin greenish colored stick about three or four inches long.

"What's that?" I asked.

Scritch, scritch, scritch went Patches' tongue against my pants.

"It's a stem of hay. Alfalfa. First crop. From that field we baled last on the other place."

"How do you know all that?" I asked.

Scritch, scritch, scritch went Patches' tongue. She stopped licking my pants and turned her attention to the front of my chore coat.

"Well, I'm pretty sure it's from that last field. To be this big, it would have to be, I think," Dad said.

"Was it stuck?" I asked.

He nodded. "Wedged under the paddle at the top. I'm going to have to be more careful about putting on so much fertilizer. The hay grows. But then the stems get too big."

He tossed the alfalfa stem onto the windowsill.

Just then, I saw headlights on the hill closest to the church.

"Loretta's coming home!" I said.

"And it's time for us to get to the house for supper," Dad said.

"Bye Patches," I said.

Needles had stayed right where we left him, nose on his paws, eyes trained in our direction. When we reached the barn door, the dog rose to his feet.

My father opened the door, and Needles trotted out behind us. The dog stood still in the moonlight, his nose lifted to the wind, sniffing. The moon was not full, only a half moon, but with the snow on the ground, there was almost enough light to read by.

Instead of following us to the house as he usually did, Needles turned and headed directly for the granary.

"I wish he'd stay in the barn where it's warm," Dad said under his breath.

By now I could clearly hear the sound of Loretta's car, and before we reached the garage, she had turned the corner and parked by the house.

"You're home," Dad said as my sister opened her car door.

Loretta was wearing her three-quarter length light brown winter coat, a green patterned wool skirt and the black high heeled winter boots she had bought a few years ago. As my mother said, when Loretta went to work, she never had a hair out of place.

"I thought you'd be in the house by now," my sister said.

"Had to fix a water cup," Dad replied.

Loretta leaned into the car and brought out a paper bag.

"Would you carry this?" she said, handing me the bag.

"Want me to carry something?" Dad asked.

She reached into the car for more bags and then closed the car door.

"What's in the bags?" Dad asked.

Loretta daintily picked her way through the snow toward the house. Dad had shoveled the path, but the spiky heels on her black winter boots would sink into spots where the snow was not packed down tight.

"Christmas tree decorations," Loretta replied. "If it's not too cold tomorrow, I was hoping we could go out and cut a Christmas tree."

"Yippeeeee!" I said.

"They'll be frozen now," Dad said.

"Won't it thaw out in the barn overnight?" Loretta asked. She carefully started to make her way up the porch steps.

"Oh, sure," Dad said. "We can put it in the barn. In the corner by Dusty's pen. That's if she doesn't try to eat it."

My pony, I had discovered, liked to taste the most unlikely things. Last summer, she had eaten some of our neighbor's flowers. Mom was upset when she found out. But our neighbor, Hannah, had laughed and said if Dusty thought her cosmos tasted that good, maybe she ought to put them in a salad. Dusty also liked oranges, cake, oatmeal cookies and peanut butter cookies.

Loretta went through the porch, opened the kitchen door and went into the kitchen.

"Here," she said. "Give me the bags. Then you can take your boots and coats off."

Dad handed his bag to Loretta and reached for my bag.

A few minutes later, I stood in the kitchen by the table, staring down into one of the paper bags. Inside were several packages of what looked like cotton balls that had been pulled apart.

"What's for supper?" Dad asked.

"Meatloaf," Mom said. She was sitting in her chair by the end of the table. The kitchen smelled good. My mother had put onions in the meatloaf she was mixing together when I arrived home from school.

"And we're having mashed potatoes," I said. My mother had asked me to go to the basement to bring up some potatoes before I went out to the barn.

I reached into the paper bag.

"What's this stuff?" I asked, holding up one of the packages.

"Angel hair," Loretta said. "We're going to use it to decorate the Christmas tree."

"What's it made out of?" I wondered.

I was pretty sure that it could not actually be real hair. For one thing, it was much too white.

"Well," Loretta said, "I don't know exactly what it's made out of. Maybe it says on the package."

I turned over the package.

"Does it say?" Mom asked.

"No. It just says it's angel hair for decorating a Christmas tree."

I put the package back in the paper bag with the others.

"How do you put it on the tree?" I said.

For as long as I could remember, we had decorated our Christmas trees with lights, ornaments and tinsel.

"You have to pull the angel hair apart and then you just sort of stick it on the tree," Loretta said.

"Is it sticky? Like glue?" I asked.

"No, it's not sticky," Loretta said. "It hangs from the branches."

"Like tinsel?"

"Not like tinsel, exactly."

"But what will it look like?" I asked.

"We've got some on the Christmas tree at work," Loretta said, "and it looks like... well...let's see...it looks like...fog ...or maybe mist is a better word."

"The tree will look like it's covered with fog?" I said.

"And then when the Christmas tree lights are on you can see them shining through the angel hair," my big sister said.

She shook her head. "It's hard to describe. But once we decorate the tree with it, you'll see what I mean."

The next day, the north wind was not quite as fierce as it had been. In the afternoon, with the sun shining out of a bright blue sky, making the snow sparkle like someone had sprinkled it with diamonds, we drove over to the other place to cut a Christmas tree. The "other place" was a second farm my parents owned. They had sold off the buildings but had kept the fields. The snow was too deep to drive through, so we left the truck on the road and walked in to find a tree.

When we arrived back home again, Dad set the tree in the corner by Dusty's pen next to Thumper's cage. The rabbit sat up on his haunches to get a better look at the green tree that seemed so out of place in the barn. Every year we cut a Christmas tree and put in the barn to thaw out. But that was only once a year.

"We're gonna have to keep an eye on Dusty when we bring her in tonight," Dad said.

Later that afternoon when I brought the pony in and put her in the pen, I watched to see what she would do. Dusty put her head over the calf pen wall and started nuzzling the branches. Before I could stop her, she opened her mouth and bit off a clump of pine needles.

"Daddy!" I called. "Dusty is eating the Christmas tree!"

My father was up in front of the cows and hurried to the calf pen.

"Here," Dad said. "Stop that." He picked up the Christmas tree and backed into the barn aisle.

"Where are you going to put it now?" I asked.

"Let's see," Dad said. "I guess I'll have to put it...well, maybe I can set it by the feed box."

With the Christmas tree leaning against the south door, there wasn't much room to get by the feed box or up in front of the cows.

"It'll be all right. We can live with it until tomorrow," Dad said.

When Sunday afternoon finally arrived, my father brought the Christmas tree into the house and set it up in the tree stand that was made out of metal and shaped like the funnels Dad used to put oil or hydraulic fluid into the tractor. It was decorated with scenes of snow and trees and houses and horses and sleighs.

Every year we put the Christmas tree in front of the picture window in the living room. And every year we started with the lights. One time I asked Loretta why we always put the tree by the window. She said it was so people could see the lights from the road. When I pointed out that no one ever drove on our road at night, Loretta said it was dark when she came home on Friday night, and she liked to see the tree lights as she drove toward the house.

After that, Mom said it was my job to make sure the tree lights were plugged in before Loretta came home on Friday night. The strings of tree lights were made up of colored oblong bulbs: red, green, blue, yellow and white. Since Loretta thought the Christmas tree was so pretty from the road, a couple of times after dark while the tree was in the living room, I would walk partway down the driveway so I could see the lights.

As I stood by the back of the tree, waiting for my sister to hand the string of lights to me from her side so we could go around the tree again, I thought about last year's Christmas tree.

Everything had started out fine, but after I reached for the string of lights, my hands had started to itch. And each time I moved to the back of the tree to reach for the lights again, the itching became more intense and felt like mosquito bites all over my hands. And I knew all about mosquito bites. Whenever Dad and I went fishing after chores in the summer or on Sunday afternoons, the mosquitoes always found me. And once I got a mosquito bite, it did not stop itching for weeks. Even after the bite disappeared, the spot where it had been would still itch.

By the time we had finished with the Christmas tree lights last year, not only were my hands itching, but so was my face.

Mom wondered if my itching was because of the brand new curtains she had put up not long ago. They were white, and they had fiberglass in them. Mom said fiberglass was a material that was supposed to make the curtains last longer and not wear out so fast from being washed and from the sun shining through the window.

All I knew for sure was that before we decorated the Christmas tree, I'd never had any reason to touch the curtains. But once we started putting on the lights, I had brushed against them several times.

After that, I stayed well away from those curtains.

I had nothing to worry about this year. Mom had bought new curtains that did not contain fiberglass. She said they were called "drapes" and not "curtains." They were dark green and had a rubber coating on the back so the sun would not fade the curtains or any other furniture near the window.

We finished putting on the lights, and then it was time to hang the round colored glass ornaments. We had large blue ornaments and smaller ornaments that were red, silver and green. We also had a couple of handmade bead ornaments that Mom had bought at the church bazaar. Loretta had also bought some red and white striped candy canes this year to hang on the tree.

When the ornaments and candy canes were in place, it was time to put on the angel hair.

"Watch how I do it, and then you can help," Loretta said.

My sister opened a package and took out the white fluffy angel hair. She held it in her hands and pulled it apart. Now that it was out of the package, it looked like milkweed fluff. Loretta carefully laid the angel hair against the tree branches and stepped back to look at it.

She was right. It *did* look like fog on the tree. And the lights were very pretty shining through it.

"Now you try it," Loretta said.

I reached into the package. As soon as I pulled out a handful of the angel hair, my fingers started to itch.

I quickly dropped the angel hair and began to scratch my hands.

"Your fingers itch?" Mom asked.

My mother never helped decorate the Christmas tree because it was too difficult for her to stand up and put on ornaments without holding onto something. Dad suggested setting one of the kitchen chairs by the tree so she could lean on it, but Mom said she would rather watch.

Just then, my face started tingling, too.

"And my face. My face itches," I said.

"Your hands itch? And your face?" Loretta said.

"And my eyes," I said.

"What in the world…?" Mom said.

Loretta looked at Mom. And Mom looked at Loretta.

And then they both turned to look at me.

"Oh, no," Loretta said. "You don't suppose that stuff is made of—"

"Fiberglass," Mom said. "Maybe you'd better wash your hands and your face."

"Fiberglass?" I said. "Like the curtains?"

"Go and wash your hands and face. And don't just rinse. Suds up your hands and *wash*," Mom said.

I went to the bathroom, lathered my hands with Ivory soap and then washed my face, too.

By the time I had finished drying my face and hands, the itching had stopped.

"You'd better let me put the rest of this on the tree," Loretta said.

She turned to Mom. "On second thought, maybe we shouldn't put it on the tree at all."

"But I want to see what it looks like with angel hair on it!" I said.

"So would I," said Dad. He was sitting on the davenport, paging through the latest edition of *Hoard's Dairyman*. Dad never helped decorate the tree, but he, too, liked to watch.

Loretta had told me one time that when she and Ingman were little, Dad used to go up on the Bluff and cut a jack pine for a Christmas tree. After Loretta and Ingman went to bed on Christmas Eve, Dad and Mom would decorate it, and when my sister and brother came downstairs on Christmas Day, there would be the prettiest little Christmas tree in whole wide world.

Mom looked at me and frowned. "We can have angel hair on the tree only under one condition," she said.

"What's that?" I asked.

"You have to promise not to touch the Christmas tree," she said.

I looked at the Christmas tree. I never really had a reason to go close to it once it was decorated—except to plug it in before I went out to the barn Friday afternoon. But I did not have to touch the tree to plug it in.

"Do you *promise*?" Mom asked.

"Yes," I said.

To tell you the truth, I was not eager to have my hands and face itch like that again.

Loretta finished putting the angel hair on the tree. With the angel hair spread over the branches, the tree really did look like it was covered with mist.

"Pretty," Dad said.

"Very pretty," Mom said.

For the rest of the time our Christmas tree was in the living room, as long as I did not brush up against it, everything was fine.

When Christmas was over and we were ready to take down the tree on New Year's Day, my sister gathered up the angel hair and said she was going to throw it away.

"It was pretty for once. But it's not worth it," she said, stuffing the angel hair into a paper bag.

"I hope you didn't pay a lot of money for that," Mom said.

"Who cares if I did?" Loretta replied.

As Loretta continued to stuff angel hair into the paper bag, my mother started to smile. The smile progressed to a twitter and soon she was laughing so hard that tears were trickling down her cheeks.

"What's so funny?" I asked.

"Fiberglass," she gasped.

"What's funny about fiberglass?"

"They say it's supposed to make things last a lot longer. Didn't help my curtains, though. Didn't help the angel hair, either."

After I'd thought about it for a bit, I could see what Mom meant.

No, the fiberglass did not make the curtains *or* the angel hair last longer.

Not with me in the house.

☀☀☀☀☀☀☀☀☀☀☀☀☀☀☀☀☀☀☀☀☀

~ 11 ~
No Fun At All

We only had a few days left of Christmas vacation, and I had not seen my best friend, Vicki, since the bus ride home from school the day vacation started. I had gotten permission from Mom to call this morning to see if Vicki could come over to my house. Her mom said she could, and her dad said he would bring her.

More snow had fallen a few days ago, and as I stood next to the window in the living room, watching for their car, the cow pasture across the driveway looked as smooth as white frosting on a cake. The snow was deep enough to cover the longer tufts of grass the cows would not eat that had grown up around flattened piles of cow manure. I never could figure out why some people called them cow pies.

My mother's chair had been moved back closer to the wood stove so there would be room for the Christmas tree. She was working on embroidering a pillowcase.

"What are you two going to do?" Mom asked. "Go sledding?"

"Maybe," I said.

Technically, we would not be sledding in the cow pasture. A long time ago, I had discovered that a sled did not work very well in the deep snow. And Mom did not want me to slide down the driveway, seeing as she always worried that a car might come along just when I reached the bottom of the hill. Under the right conditions, when the snow on the driveway had been worn smooth, my sled would go all the way across the road. I had tried pointing out to my mother that the only traffic on our road, especially in the winter, was either Dad, Loretta, Ingman or the milk truck. But it made no difference.

Just then I saw a car come over the hill closest to the church.

I hurried into the kitchen, and a few minutes later, I watched through the window as Vicki got out of the car. She stood with the door open, talking to her dad. Then she shut the door, and while she walked toward the house, her dad backed up and headed down the driveway. In the meantime, my mother got up from her chair, fitted the cuffs of her crutches over her forearms and made her way into the kitchen. As Vicki took her coat off, my mother settled herself into the chair at her end of the table.

"What are we going to do this afternoon?" Vicki asked.

"We could get my toboggan out," I said.

Vicki looked at me. I knew the sparkle in her blue eyes. It meant she was getting a grand idea.

"You've got a pair of skis, don't you?" she said.

"Yes. But I'm not very good with them yet."

I had gotten the skis for Christmas. I did not know exactly what kind of skis they were. Mom said they were not like the cross-country skis she had when she was a kid because they were longer than that. Loretta said they had longer skis in the store that the man said were good for going down big hills at ski resorts. The shorter skis, he said, would be just right for me. I have no idea what he had meant by "just right" because when I tried to ski with them, I kept falling down.

"Actually," I said, "I can't even make it a few feet."

"Where have you tried them?" Vicki asked.

"In the pasture across the driveway," I said.

"What happened?" Vicki wondered.

"I fell down."

"A lot?"

"A lot."

"It's going to take time to learn how to use them," my mother said. "I hope, after your sister went to all the trouble to get them for you, that you keep trying and don't just let them gather dust."

"What about if we try skiing?" Vicki asked.

"Okay," I said.

I hoped that I sounded more enthusiastic than I felt.

"But one of us will have to do something else. It's only one pair," I said.

"No, we won't," Vicki said.

My mother frowned. She, too, knew the sparkly look in Vicki's eyes.

"And why won't one of you have to do something else? You've also got a toboggan," Mom said.

"Because," Vicki said, pulling out a kitchen chair and flopping into it triumphantly. "We can each use a ski!"

"What?" I said.

"What?" Mom asked.

"We can each use a ski!"

"How are you each going to use a ski?" Mom asked.

Vicki looked back and forth between my mother and me.

"We can put one foot in front of the other one. Like this," she said.

Vicki stood up and demonstrated how we could stand on the ski, the toe of one foot to the heel of the other.

"Oh!" I said. "I see! And then we can..."

"You can't each use just one pole for balance," my mother interrupted.

"We can't?" I said.

"Why not?" Vicki said.

"It won't work very well."

"How do you know?" Vicki did not say it in a mean way. She really wanted to know how my mother knew.

"Because I've skied before," Mom said.

If it had been any other situation, the astonishment on Vicki's face would have made me laugh out loud.

"You have?"

My mother nodded. "I used to ski when I went to school at Norton."

"You did?" Vicki said.

"So that's how I know that using one pole won't work very well," Mom said.

Vicki flopped down in the chair again.

"I know!" she said, sitting up straight. "Twine string! You have lots of that in the barn, don't you?"

We did, indeed, have a whole barrel full of used twine in the barn.

"Well, we can tie a twine string to the front of the ski and hold onto that!" Vicki said.

The sparkle was back in her eyes.

"Hey!" I said. "We could!"

My mother shook her head. "Now hold on just a minute. I don't think that's such a good idea."

"Sure it is," Vicki said. "It will give us something to hold onto. And we can steer with it."

"You can't steer skis with twine string," Mom said.

Vicki thought for a moment. "Even if we can't, we can still use it to hold onto for balance."

"What about the fence?" Mom asked. "What if you run into the fence?"

My mother was always worried I would run into the fence. When I started tobogganing in the pasture, I thought it would make her feel better because she would not have to worry about me sliding out into the road. But then I found out she was worried about me sliding into the fence.

"The skis won't go that far, will they?" Vicki asked.

"I don't think so," I said.

"You never know," Mom said.

"Please, Mrs. Ralph? Can we please try it?" Vicki asked.

"Please?" I said.

My mother tapped her fingers against the table. "Well…"

"Please?" Vicki said.

"Only if you promise not to go so fast that you end up by the fence," Mom said.

"We could go the other way," Vicki said.

"The other way?" Mom said.

"What other way?" I said.

"We could start out by the driveway and cut down toward the creek," Vicki said.

As I thought about it, I could see that cutting across the hill might actually work.

"No!" Mom said.

"Why not?" Vicki asked.

"Why not?" I said.

My mother looked horrified at the very thought. "The creek is down there!"

The creek was fed by the spring that ran along the driveway and a spring that came out of the neighbor's cow pasture. The two springs met and flowed into a culvert under the road. The creek was not much of a creek, as far as I could see. It was a couple of feet wide at the most.

"It's not a very big creek," Vicki said.

"But if you go into it, you'll get wet," Mom said.

"So?" I said.

"You don't want to be wet outside in the winter. It's too cold!" Mom said.

I did not want to admit it, but I knew my mother had a point. Sometimes the calves splashed milk on my leg, and once or twice I had splashed myself while rinsing out the milkers. On the way to house with a wet pant leg, it felt like the cloth was freezing onto my skin.

"Okay," I said. "We'll start out by the driveway and go down that way instead of starting up by the other fence."

The hill by the neighbor's fence was a higher hill than the hill by the driveway and would make a dandy skiing hill. But if my mother was going to worry about the fence by the driveway so much she wouldn't let us go, then the shorter hill was better than nothing.

"That will be fine. I just don't want you trying to ski down the higher hill so I have to worry about the fence. Or skiing down the hill by the driveway on a diagonal so I have to worry about the creek," Mom said.

"Okay, Mrs. Ralph. That's what we'll do," Vicki said. She stood up and reached for her winter coat.

"Have you got a hat and mittens?" my mother asked.

"Yup," Vicki said. She reached into the big pocket on one side of her coat and brought out a stocking cap. She reached into the other pocket and brought out a pair of mittens.

"And what boots do you have?" Mom inquired.

"Moooooother!" I said.

Vicki held up one foot. "I've got these on," she said.

She was wearing a pair of winter boots that looked like black leather and came halfway up to her knee. The boots, I knew, were lined with fleece. Her jeans were tucked into the top of the boots.

"You'll be fine with those, I think," Mom said. "And your pant legs are tucked in, too, so you won't be as likely to get snow down your boots."

I headed for the porch. Vicki turned to follow me.

"Just remember," Mom said. "Don't ski down the high hill on the south side, and—"

"—don't ski down the other hill on a diagonal," I said.

"Right," Mom said.

I opened the porch door. Vicki went out ahead of me, and I closed the door behind us.

"Yikes," Vicki said in a whisper. "Your mom sure does worry a lot."

"I know," I whispered back.

"She's a worrywart, isn't she," Vicki whispered.

I put on my coat and boots and hat and mittens, and then Vicki and I left the house.

"Boy," Vicki said after we were outside and were headed for the machine shed to get my skis. "Your mom must not have had any fun at all when she was little, so that's why she doesn't want us to have any fun."

"I think so, too," I said.

Vicki and I retrieved the skis from where I had put them in the machine shed, and then we went to the barn for a couple of pieces of twine string. When I took the cover off the barrel, the tangy odor of the twine filled my nose and made me think of lemons and lemonade. During the summer while we were baling hay, we would store a jug of lemonade in the twine box on the baler.

A few minutes later, Vicki and I walked part way down the driveway and crawled through the fence.

"The other hill would be better," Vicki said, gazing across the pasture.

"I know," I said. "But maybe if we do all right on this hill and Mom sees that it's not dangerous, she'll let us use the other hill."

Vicki and I both turned to look toward the house. My mother was standing in the living room by the picture window, leaning on her crutches. I don't know how long she had been watching us.

Vicki and I both waved. Mom waved back. Then we turned our attention to the skis.

"If we tie the string with a slip knot around the top part where it curves up—"

"—the knot will tighten when we pull back on it, so it will stay where it belongs," I finished.

A little while later, we had tied the twine strings to our satisfaction.

"I'll go first," Vicki said.

She put one foot into the binding, a kind of a half a shoe that you could slide your boot into. She put her other foot in front.

Holding tightly onto the string, she leaned forward and, slowly, the ski began moving down the hill, taking Vicki with it.

All at once, I wondered how she was going to stop when she reached the bottom of the slope. I'd never had that problem myself because I had never made it to the bottom.

"How am I going to stop?" Vicki yelled over her shoulder.

"I don't know," I yelled back.

When Vicki reached the bottom of the hill, she stopped abruptly, lost her balance and fell over sideways into the snow. From where I stood, I could hear her giggling.

"What happened?" I said.

Vicki sat up and turned to face me. "There's a little dip at the bottom. The ski came over that and pushed into the snow. Try it. It's fun. You'll see."

I put my right foot into the ski, put my left foot in front and took a firm hold on the twine string. I leaned forward—and then I was gliding down the hill. At the bottom, where there was a dip, the ski came up, over, and then dug into the snow. Since I had watched Vicki go down, I was ready for it.

Vicki waited until I had landed in the snow. She got up and held out her hand to help me.

"That's fun!" I said.

"See?" Vicki replied. "I told you."

"Now we've got to get back up the hill," I said.

"I know," Vicki said. "And that's not going to be so much fun."

The snow in the cow pasture was knee deep on both of us.

"I'll go first and you come right in my footsteps. We'll make a path that way, and maybe it will be easier to get up the next time," Vicki said.

Feeling as if I were trying to wade through very cold water, I followed my friend up the hill.

"Whewwww!" Vicki said when we reached the top. "I'm glad the hill isn't any bigger than what it is."

"Me, too," I said.

I looked toward the house. My mother had sat down in her chair by the window. I waved.

"Is your Mom still watching?" Vicki asked.

"Yup," I said.

Vicki turned and waved, too.

I lost count of the number of times we skied down the hill and trudged back up through the snow. After a while, I noticed that the sun had moved much lower in the sky.

"Are you hungry?" I said.

"Starved," Vicki said.

"Maybe Loretta will make some hot chocolate for us. And there's cookies, too," I said.

"Yum!" Vicki said.

We climbed through the fence to the driveway and went to the barn where we untied the twine strings and put them back in the twine barrel. Then we put the skis in the machine shed and headed for the house. We took turns brushing the snow off each other before we went into the porch.

"What smells so good?" Vicki asked when I opened the kitchen door.

My big sister stood by the stove, beating something in a pan with the eggbeater.

"I made hot cocoa," Loretta said, turning toward us. "And there's cookies, too. Peanut butter."

A plate of peanut butter cookies sat on the table.

"You were out there quite a while," Loretta said. "I was sure you'd be getting hungry."

"I'm *starving*," Vicki said as she helped herself to two cookies. "What's for supper? Any chance it's that really good soup you make?"

Mom put her hand up to her mouth but wasn't quite able to hide her smile. Loretta bit her lips and turned back toward the hot chocolate.

Personally, I couldn't see what was so funny about being hungry.

"Do you think your mom would let you stay for supper?" I asked.

Vicki shrugged. "Maybe."

Loretta reached into the cupboard for four ceramic coffee mugs and began to pour the hot chocolate. Some of the mugs were bright yellow and some were bright green. Yellow was my mother's favorite color because it was the color of sunshine. My sister set a mug of hot chocolate in front of each of us and kept one for herself.

"So," my mother said after a sip of hot cocoa. "I see you didn't venture any farther than the hill by the driveway."

I finished chewing my bite of cookie. "You told us not to!"

Vicki set her mug back on the table.

"That was so much fun. When you come to my house, bring your skis. We can try skiing on the what-cha-ma-call it," she said.

"What-cha-ma-call it?" Mom said.

"What's a what-cha-ma-call it?" Loretta asked.

"You know," Vicki said. "That place you've talked about. The hog—hogs—"

"Hogsback," my mother said.

"Yeah, that's it," Vicki said.

When my mother was growing up, relatives of hers had lived on a farm that was now part of the farm where Vicki lived. An old house was still there, although no one lived in it. And the barn was there yet, too, as well as a couple of sheds. You could see daylight through the roof of the barn, but the horse stalls were still downstairs where the workhorses had been kept. And there were some pieces of harness in the barn and a couple of horse collars.

Vicki's house was only a mile and a half away, but the farm was pretty much flat— except for the Hogsback, which really was not much of a hill.

"You didn't hardly fall down at all, that I could see," Loretta said. She leaned against the counter, holding her cup of hot chocolate.

"You were watching?" I said.

"For a little while," my sister replied. "I thought it looked like fun."

When my sister was a girl, I knew she had climbed trees and rode the workhorses and had gone sledding—but I had never seen her do any of those things. Except for climb a tree. One Christmas we had climbed a big pine tree at the back of the farm and had cut off the top for a Christmas tree.

Vicki looked at my mother. "Mrs. Ralph, do you think we'd be able to ski on the Hogsback?"

"Oh, yes. You'll have fun on the Hogsback," Mom said.

"I will never forget the time," she continued, setting her cup of hot chocolate on the table, "going sledding there when I was a kid. I thought we were goners."

"You went sledding?" I said. I could feel my eyebrows drawing together into a frown.

"Many times," Mom said. "And don't look at me like I have suddenly grown two heads. I did have fun when I was a kid, you know."

"What happened?" Vicki asked.

"Well," my mother said, "we, ahhhh, we, well … we ran into a tree."

"You did what?" I said.

"A tree!" Vicki exclaimed.

"Yes, we ran into a tree," Mom said. "With the sled. I suppose there's not much for trees around there now. Wasn't much for trees around there then, either, I guess. Except for that one."

"Did you get hurt?" Loretta asked.

Mom shook her head. "Just the front of the runner caught the edge of the tree. We flew sideways. Face down in the snow. Took my breath away."

"What happened then?" Vicki asked.

"It was time to quit. The sun was going down," Mom said. "I was afraid to tell my mother, though, that's for sure."

"How come?" I said.

"Because she worried so much about everything," Mom said. "It always seemed to me that she never wanted me to have any fun."

"Is that why you worry so much?" Vicki asked.

My mother looked startled. "Maybe it is." She paused and reached for her cup of hot cocoa. "I always swore to myself I wasn't going to be like that, but I guess I haven't been very successful, have I …"

Her voiced trailed away.

I looked at Vicki and she looked at me.

Maybe my mother understood more about having fun than I thought she did.

During all the times I had been sledding and tobogganing, I had never come anywhere *close* to a tree.

Imagine that—Mom actually ran into a tree and ended up face down in the snow.

****

~ 12 ~
Wake Up!

Today was the last day of Christmas vacation. School started again tomorrow. I had been hoping we would get a big snowstorm so we would have one more day off from school. But I knew that wasn't going to happen. Dad said it was much too cold to snow. As I went upstairs to put my pajamas on, I could hear the north wind whistling around the eaves. It was a sad and lonesome sound, like the wind was crying, the way the barn cats cried when something happened to their kittens and they could not find them.

I reached the top of the steps and paused, listening to the wind. Then I turned on the lamp beside my bed and went to the closet to find my pajamas. The pink and blue flowered flannel shirt and pants were icy cold, and I shivered as I buttoned up the shirt. Putting on the pajama bottoms wasn't any better, but if I thought my pajamas felt cold against my skin, I knew the sheets were going to be worse. There were no heat vents upstairs. Mom said when her Norwegian grandfather had built the four-room log cabin after the other house burned down, there was no need for heat vents. Furnaces had not yet been invented then.

Making sure that I kept my bare feet on the rag rug, I pulled back the covers, took a deep breath and crawled into bed. The sheets felt as if they had been hanging outside on the clothesline only moments before, and my teeth began to chatter as I pulled the blankets up to my chin. If I could only stand it for a couple of minutes, the sheets and blankets—not to mention my pillow—would eventually warm up.

To distract myself from thinking about my chattering teeth, I pulled one arm from beneath the blankets and reached for a book that I kept on the nightstand. I always had a book to read. This one was about a girl whose dad raised race horses, and in less than a minute, I was so caught up in the story that I paid no attention to my chattering teeth. By the time I started to feel sleepy, I discovered that the sheets and blankets were no longer icy.

I put the book on the nightstand and reached for the electric alarm clock Dad had given to me for my birthday last summer. I never knew why Dad thought an alarm clock would be a good present, but it turned out to be much better than the old windup clock I had used before. For one thing, I did not have to worry about remembering to wind it. And for another thing, it had a loud alarm impossible to ignore. The alarm on the old windup clock would only ring for a little while before the clock ran down. The electric alarm kept on screeching until I shut it off.

Mom said I was lucky we had electricity in the house so I could use the alarm clock. The REA had only come into being in the 1940s, she said. When I asked what "R-E-A" meant, she said it was the Rural Electric Association.

I made sure the alarm clock was set for five-thirty so I would have time to go out and help Dad feed the cows and start milking before I had to get ready for school. The bus came at 7:20 a.m., and as long as I was in the house by 6:30 or twenty minutes to seven, I would have plenty of time to wash up, eat breakfast and get dressed for school. Mom said breakfast was important, and she insisted that I eat toast and cereal or toast and eggs before I got on the bus. Toast was my favorite. We had all kinds of lovely homemade blackberry and strawberry jam and pin cherry and chokecherry jelly in the basement that Mom had made last summer.

I pushed the little switch into the "on" position, turned off the lamp and pulled the covers up to my chin again. Now that the sheets and blankets were warmed up, I knew I would be able to fall asleep. I turned over onto my left side and settled onto the pillow.

This was no good. My left ear felt like it was going to explode when it was against the pillow.

I turned over onto my right side.

Oh, yes. This was better. Much better.

Just to make sure, I turned over onto my left side again. Sure enough, my left ear now felt like I was underwater.

I turned back onto my ride side. And just like that, my left ear felt better.

And here Mom thought I had outgrown ear infections. A few days after Vicki and I had gone skiing, I came down with an ear infection that settled in my left ear—just as it always did. When I was a very little girl, I suffered from frequent ear infections. Dad said I came by it honestly, because he used to get ear infections all the time, too, when he was little.

As I settled down on the pillow, I realized that up until now, I had not noticed whether it made much difference which side I slept on. Before this, my head had felt tight and congested all the way around.

Right before I had come upstairs, Mom said I should probably stay home from school tomorrow, but since it was the first day back after vacation, I wanted to go. If you missed out on the first day back, then it seemed like it took an awfully long time to catch up. There was a difference between a snow day when no one went to school and a day when everyone else went to school but you stayed home sick...

It seemed as if I had been asleep for only a few minutes when suddenly, I felt as if something had hit me. Except—how could that be? I was in my room, under the quilts and blankets. I must have been dreaming.

Ka-WHAP!

There it was again.

My eyes popped open. The room was dark. Well, not completely dark. A little light filtered up the stairs from the kitchen. Mom and Dad must not have gone to bed yet. Otherwise the kitchen light would not still be on.

But wait. What was that I could smell? It smelled like ... well ... it smelled like coffee.

Coffee? At this time of night?

What was Mom doing making coffee *now*? She always said Norwegians liked their coffee, but even my mother did not make coffee at night. Not usually. Except for that one time during the summer when there was a bad thunderstorm. She had awakened Dad, and Ingman, too, and had insisted they go out—in the middle of the night—to shut the big barn door where we loaded hay into the mow so the hay would not get wet. But that was the only time I knew of when she had made coffee at night—

Ka-plink!

Something bounced off the bed and landed on the floor.

I sat up. "What was that?"

"FINALLY!" I heard a voice exclaim.

And then I realized I could hear something else: a loud, insistent buzzing.

What was *that*?

Oh. Right. The alarm clock.

I reached over and shut off the alarm, and then I twisted around to look toward the stairs where I could see a shadowy figure.

It was my mother on her hands and knees at the head of the steps. She was holding a shoe in one hand.

Because of the polio, Mom could only crawl up the steps on her hands and knees.

"Did you throw something at me Mom?"

"YES I threw something!"

"But why?" I asked, blinking in the sudden glare when I turned on the lamp

"Because your alarm went off!"

Boy, I thought as I threw back the covers, *Mom must think I'm deaf or something.*

"You didn't have to throw things at me," I grumbled as I swung my legs over the side of the bed.

"How else was I going to get you to wake up?"

"You could have yelled."

Mom sighed. "Tried that. Didn't work."

As I got out of bed, I noticed the floor was littered with shoes, slippers, books—anything that had been within my mother's reach from the top of the stairs.

"How long were you yelling and throwing things?" I asked.

"When you didn't shut off your alarm after the first minute, I started up the steps. And you know how long that takes," Mom replied.

I did, indeed, know. It took my mother a long time to reach the top of the stairs. Which meant my alarm must have been screeching for at least five minutes. But how could that be?

After Dad had given me the alarm clock for my birthday, the first time I used it, I had practically leaped out of bed. With my heart pounding, I had pressed the switch, thinking there was no way I could ever sleep through the alarm.

"Okay," Mom said. "You're up. I'm going back downstairs."

I found a thick pair of socks and put on my pants and a sweatshirt. Then I headed downstairs, too.

I stopped at the head of the steps to look out my bedroom window, but I couldn't see much because the glass was covered with frost.

"Did it get below zero?" I asked when I reached the bottom of the steps.

My mother had sat down by the table with a cup of coffee.

"Yes," she said.

I walked over to look at the thermometer mounted outside the north window. The furnace grate occupied the floor directly below, so only a little bit of frost covered the very top of the windowpane.

"It's ten degrees below zero!" I said.

"I know," Mom said. "Maybe you'd better bring your coat and boots in from the porch to let them warm up."

I went out into the porch for my coat and boots and hat and mittens. It was almost as cold in the porch as it was outside. I knew I could leave my coat and boots on the furnace grate for a few minutes without scorching anything. When my boots started to smell like hot rubber, then I would know it was time to take everything off the grate.

"How does your ear feel this morning?" Mom asked.

I had been so busy trying to wake up that I hadn't yet thought about my ear.

"Well," I said. "It feels plugged. Like I've got cotton in it."

"Does it hurt?"

I paused to consider. "Not really. It just mostly feels plugged up."

"It must be if you couldn't hear that alarm!" Mom said.

In a minute, I could smell hot rubber, so I took my boots and coat off the furnace grate and began to get dressed. There was hardly anything nicer than putting on warm boots and a warm coat when it was cold outside. If I put my boots and coat on without warming them up first, it was as bad as getting into bed at night.

"Don't stay out there too long," Mom said as I pulled open the kitchen door. "Since you've been sick lately, I think it's especially important for you to eat breakfast before you leave for school."

"Yes, Mom," I said.

A minute later I stepped out onto the porch. The cold air felt like pins poking my nose as I walked toward the barn. When I opened the barn door, the first thing I saw was Needles curled up on his burlap sacks.

"Did Needles sleep in the barn last night?" I asked. Dad was crouched by a cow, putting on the milker. He shook his head.

"Nope. He stayed in the granary. I made sure he came in the barn with me right away."

Needles got up from the pile of burlap, turned around in a circle, and flopped down again.

"How's your ear today?" Dad asked.

"Plugged," I said. "I couldn't hear my alarm clock."

"You couldn't?"

"Mom had to come upstairs and wake me up."

"She did?"

"Yeah," I said. "She stood at the top of the steps and threw things at me until I woke up."

"Things?" Dad asked.

"Shoes, books. Whatever she could reach. She was yelling, too. I think it was a shoe that finally hit me."

Dad shook his head. "Must be some plugged up ear if you couldn't hear *that* alarm."

My father crossed the gutter channel. "Do you feel sick?"

"No, not really. It's just that my head feels like it's...well...like it's..."

I spied the little green tin of udder cream sitting next to the bucket with the washcloth and iodine solution. During the winter, Dad rubbed udder cream on the cows when he was finished milking.

"My head feels like it's stuffed full of udder cream," I said.

"I know the feeling," Dad said.

Not that I had anything against udder cream. I loved the way it smelled—like wintergreen. But when it was cold in the winter, the udder cream was so stiff you almost could not scoop it out of the tin. Sometimes Dad had to let it sit in the bucket of warm water for a while to soften it up.

That night, my ear still felt plugged. I had made it through the school day all right, except sometimes when people talked to me, I had to turn my "good" ear toward them and ask them to repeat what they said. Just before I went upstairs, Mom asked if she should plan on waking me up in the morning instead of me setting the alarm.

"I can't believe you couldn't hear that," she said. "I almost jump out of my skin every morning when it goes off. And I'm clear down in the kitchen."

"Maybe I'll be able to hear it tomorrow," I said.

"But what if you don't?" Mom asked.

"How is she going to find out if her ear is getting better and whether she can hear the alarm if she doesn't set it?" Dad asked.

"Well," Mom said. "I guess you do have a point."

As it turned out, I was not able to hear the alarm the next morning, and once again, my mother had to throw books and shoes at me. She even ran out of ammunition and had to take off her own shoes before I woke up.

The same thing happened the next morning. And the next. And the next.

After a while, my mother would remind me every night before I went upstairs to leave plenty of books and shoes by the top of the steps.

What a relief when my ear cleared up and I could hear the alarm again.

Waking up to the alarm, I decided, was a whole lot nicer than waking up to slippers and books and shoes.

Even if I did have to wait a minute or two for my heart to stop pounding.

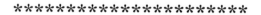

~13~
An A-Peeling Job

Through the inky blackness of a winter's night, the barn lights cast pools of butter-yellow on the snow underneath the barn windows. Dad had gone out to the barn a while ago, but I had stayed in the house to help my mother clear the table and to stack the dishes by the sink. I thought it was a whole lot of fun to help Dad with the milking—especially after I had overheard him tell my mother how much easier it was to milk by himself when he had someone to carry milk if Ingman was working.

On my way across the yard, I stopped for a moment, breathing in the clear, cold air. The clicking and clacking of a train on the tracks a couple of miles to the south was the only sound I could hear, besides the wheezing and whirring of the milker pump.

Any second now, the train would reach the "whistle post" and the engineer would blow the whistle to let cars know that the train was approaching the crossing. I had never noticed the little white signs with a black "W" on them along the train tracks until Dad had pointed them out. "When they get to the whistle posts, the engineer knows it's time to blow the whistle for the crossing," he had said.

I was about to start walking toward the barn again when I heard the train whistle begin to blow. *Whewww-oooo...Whewww-oooo... Whewww-ooooooo...* There were a couple of crossings not far away, so I knew the train engineer would blow the whistle many times before the train went on its way toward the next town up the line. *Whewww-oooo...Whewww-oooo...Whewww-ooooooo...*

The whistle made it sound as if the train were in the field next to the barn. The train did not sound this close during the summertime. I had asked Dad about it once, and he had said that sound travels better through cold air and over snow.

I reached up with my mitten to rub the tip of my nose, certain that if I touched it with my bare fingers, it would feel like an ice cube. In the short amount of time I had been listening to the train, the cold air had seeped through my barn coat. I hunched my shoulders and started walking toward the barn again.

By the time I reached the door, I was thinking about how nice it was going to feel to get inside out of the cold night air.

When I opened the door, I forgot all about feeling cold.

Next to the gutter channel by Dusty's pen sat a contraption that looked like a log mounted on legs. Hanging from the top was a blade with a handle on each end. Three fence posts were stacked on the floor beside it, two on the bottom and one cradled on top between the other two. Except they weren't really fence posts. Not yet. They still had all of their gray-brown bark.

I walked down the barn aisle to where Dad was putting a milker on a cow. A bucket of milk sat in the center of the aisle.

"What's that funny-looking thing by Dusty's pen?" I asked as I looked into the milker bucket to see how much there was. The milker bucket was not quite half full, which was enough to fill the milk pail once. If the milker bucket was full to the top, sometimes I had to make three trips to the milk house.

I picked up the bucket and poured the milk into the pail. I could carry a half-full milker, but it was still easier to handle the pail.

"What thing?" Dad asked, crossing the gutter channel.

"That," I said pointing to the contraption. I knew very well Dad knew what I was talking about and that he was only trying to tease me.

My father smiled, causing the creases beside his mouth to grow deeper. "That's my post-peeling holder."

"What's a post peeling holder?"

"Something to hold the fence posts while I peel the bark off them," Dad said.

"And what's that thing hanging from the top?"

"It's called a drawknife. You pull it toward you to peel the bark off," he said.

"But what's it doing in the barn?"

Dad stepped across the gutter channel again to check the milker. "I brought it in the barn because it's warmer in here than it is in the shed."

My father stepped into the center aisle again. "I figure I can throw some posts on the pickup to keep me busy for the afternoon and then take 'em back when I'm done. Besides, this way, I can just sweep the bark into the gutter and haul it out when I clean the barn."

I wanted to ask more questions, but I also knew I had to keep up with the milkers. I picked up the pail of milk, and the barn cats, who were crouched in strategic places in the aisle, all rose to their feet and trotted to the cat dish ahead of me. Once again, Needles was curled up on the pile of burlap bags Dad put in the corner for him underneath Thumper's cage. Sometimes, if the weather was not too cold, the dog would come outside with me when I carried a pail of milk. When I returned to the barn, he would come back inside with me.

Tonight, Needles never moved when I opened the barn door.

Inside the milk house it felt warm and toasty. Dad had plugged in the electric space heater that he used to keep the water pipes from freezing. If the pipes froze, Dad would not be able to wash the milkers in the morning or clean out the bulk tank. He also would have to spend time thawing out the pipes.

I climbed the wooden steps Dad had built so it was easier to dump milk into the stainless steel bulk tank. Before we got the bulk tank, we used to dump our milk into milk cans that sat in a concrete tank full of water to cool the milk.

While I waited for the milk to finish draining through the strainer pad, I wondered if I could talk Dad into showing me how the drawknife worked. Was it really possible that you could pull the knife along the bark and the bark would peel right off the logs?

I dumped the rest of the milk in the pail, made sure the milk house door was closed tightly behind me and hurried back to the barn.

"Cold out there, isn't it," Dad said as I set the empty milk pail down in the middle of the barn aisle.

"Daddy…"

"What, kiddo?"

"Would you show me how the drawknife works?"

Dad reached up to adjust his chore cap. "Funny you should say that. I was going to ask if you wanted me to show you how the drawknife works."

"Really?"

"It'll be a couple of minutes before the next cow is done, so I think we've got time."

Dad turned, walked to his log-peeling stand and bent down to pick up one of the posts.

"The first thing you gotta do is make sure you have a post to peel," he said, putting the post in between two big spikes he had driven into the top of the stand.

"What are the nails for?" I asked.

"To keep the post from slipping off one side or the other while you're peeling," Dad said.

He picked up the drawknife. "See? You hold one handle in each hand. And you put the knife against the post and pull it toward you."

As Dad pulled the drawknife toward him, a long section of bark peeled off and fell to the floor. The sweet, pungent odor of pine pitch was like the smell of the jack pines on hot summer days when we drove to the other place to see how the hay was drying and then went north on the dirt road to check for dewberries in an old field no longer planted to crops. Bumble bees and honey bees buzzed among the wildflowers and jack pine growing along the edge of the field filled the air with the scent of pine pitch.

"Why do you use pine trees for fence posts?" I asked. Small stands of pines had been planted around the farm in certain places to stop the soil from washing away.

"We don't have enough of the right kind of oak trees that I can use oak logs for fence posts. So I have to use pine. Next spring, I'm going to take them and have them treated with creosote," Dad said.

"Isn't that the stuff that makes the fence posts smell funny?" I asked.

He nodded. "That's the stuff."

The fence posts treated with creosote, I knew, smelled bitter, the way new blacktop smells bitter. Sometimes the posts had so much creosote in them that it sweated out in black beads and rolled down the sides.

"What's creosote for?" I asked.

"It makes the fence posts so they don't rot off in the ground. Our fences wouldn't be much good if the posts rot off."

As Dad talked, he continued to peel off bark that fell in long strips around his feet.

"That looks like fun," I said.

My father shrugged. "Well, I don't know how much 'fun' it is, but it's not very hard to do. Here. You give it a try."

Dad moved away from the fence post and handed me the drawknife. "Put it against the bark and pull it toward you."

I took the handles of the drawknife, one in each hand, and slid the blade along the bark.

Nothing happened.

"You've got to tip it toward the post a little," Dad said.

I took a firmer grip on the drawknife and tried again.

This time, a tiny piece of bark peeled off.

"I did it! I did it!"

"Yup, kiddo. Ya did," he said. "You keep working at it. I've got to go check my milkers."

Once again, I pressed the drawknife against the bark of the fence post, and this time, a long sliver of bark peeled off.

I had been concentrating so hard, that a few minutes later I was surprised to see Dad pouring milk into the kitty dish right beside me.

"Why didn't you tell me there was milk to carry?" I said. I hung the drawknife back on the stand.

My father shrugged. "You were busy."

"It's so much fun!" I said.

As soon as Dad put his hand on the barn door latch, Needles rose to his feet from his napping spot on the burlap bags.

"Don't you think it's too cold outside?" Dad asked.

Needles wagged his tail. I waited for the dog to come out, and then I closed the door and followed my father to the milk house.

"What fencing are you going to do?" I asked.

Dad kept all of the cow pasture fences in tip-top shape. "I'd rather fix the fence than chase the cows," he always said.

"There's different places around the farm with those old posts. I'm not going to rebuild the whole fence, I guess, just replace some posts," he said.

Dad opened the milk house door, and I followed him inside.

"Could I do another post? I've almost got this one done."

Dad climbed the set of wooden steps, lifted the milker bucket and poured some of the milk into the strainer. I could barely lift a full milker bucket to pour milk into the milk pail. Dad made it look like handling a full milker bucket was as easy as pouring glass of milk into the strainer.

"Sure," he said. He emptied out the last of the milk. "You can peel all the posts you want."

Dad and I headed back to the barn. Needles was waiting for us by the barn door.

"I told you it was cold out here," Dad said to the dog.

Needles looked up at Dad and wagged his feathery tail.

"What do you want me to do with the post when I'm finished?" I asked.

I closed the barn door behind us. Needles went to his pile of feed sacks, collapsed, and put his nose into his tail.

"Just leave the posts right here. I'll carry 'em out to the pile tomorrow," Dad said.

I finished the first post, took it off Dad's post-peeling stand, laid it on the floor, and put another one on the stand. The barn kitties sat with their tails curled around their front paws, following the strips of bark with their eyes as they fell to floor.

While I peeled, I kept track of what Dad was doing. When there was a milker bucket to be dumped, I hung up the drawknife and carried the milk to the milkhouse.

By the time we were ready to feed the claves, I had finished all three posts.

"You're done with those so soon?" Dad asked as he began to fill up the calf pails with warm milk. I had already mixed up the milk replacer.

"Yes," I said.

"You know," Dad said. "I have to get all of those posts finished by spring. It'll take a couple months to get them treated with creosote. I'm hoping I'll have them back by the time I want to fence next fall."

"You have to get them all done?" I asked.

The pile of fence posts by the machine shed was much taller than me.

Dad nodded. "If you can keep peeling posts for the rest of the winter while you're waiting to carry milk, it would make things a whole lot easier."

"It would?"

"I could use the time to do something else."

"Like what?"

"Oh, I don't know. Fix the barn cleaner if I need to, for one thing." Dad set the milker bucket on the floor.

"Want me to help you carry the pails?" he asked.

"Would you?"

Dad and Ingman could carry four calf pails at once, but I could only carry two. I had to set them in front of the manger by twos until I had all the buckets there. Then, as fast I could, I would set the buckets in the manger and try to keep the calves from stealing milk from each other. Some calves drank fast, and when they were finished, they would push aside their neighbor and finish off that bucket, too.

When the calves were all drinking from their pails, Dad went up into the mow to throw down hay for the cows. Some of the calves were so enthusiastic that after they were finished, they gave the pail a shove with their noses and sent it clattering over the manger and onto the concrete. I watched as the calves finished their milk, then I picked up all of the pails, rinsed them out and stacked them in the corner by Dusty's pen.

The peeled bark was still on the floor yet where it had fallen every which way from the drawknife. If I made a mess like that in the house, I knew Mom would be really mad. If I even so much as accidentally dropped a piece of popcorn in the living room, my mother would get upset.

I picked up the big broom that we used to sweep the mangers and pushed the bark into the gutter channel. As Dad crossed the aisle on his way to feed hay to the cows on the other side, I finished sweeping up the last of the bark.

"See how handy that is?" he said. "If I was peeling posts in the shed, I'd be freezing to death while I was at it, and I would still have to figure out what to do with the shavings."

"Daddy? Would it *really* help if I peeled more posts?"

"Yes, kiddo, it would really help. By the time I wash the milkers and clean the barn and get the cows taken care of, the morning is gone. That only leaves me a little while in the afternoon to work at it before I've got to feed the cows again. That's if there isn't something else I've got to do."

Dusty had been watching me sweep the bark into the gutter. Dad went to the feed box and rummaged around inside. A minute later, he returned with two chunks of molasses. He put one of the chunks on his palm and held it out toward Dusty.

Faster than the blink of an eye, the pony took the treat.

"Doesn't take you long, does it," he said. He opened Thumper's door and put the other piece of molasses in front of the rabbit.

Dusty and Thumper both loved the chunks of molasses in the cow feed that had not quite gotten mixed in at the feed mill.

Dad wiped his hand on his overalls. "I know Dusty likes the molasses, but it's kind of sticky," he said.

The pony soon figured out there was no more molasses and went back to nibbling her hay.

"Now," Dad said. "Would you like me to carry in more posts tomorrow so you've got 'em handy?"

"Oh, yes, Daddy," I said.

And that was all the encouragement I needed. In the following weeks while I waited for milk to carry to the milkhouse, I peeled fence posts.

That is, I peeled posts when I was not brushing Dusty, petting Thumper or trying to think of a new trick to teach Needles.

Still, I usually managed to peel at least a couple of posts every evening.

After several weeks, my big brother said he was surprised I wasn't tired of it yet.

"You must think it's an appealing job," Ingman said.

"It is. That's what's I'm doing—peeling," I said.

He shook his head. "Appealing—a-p-p-e-a-l-i-n-g."

"What does that mean?"

"It means you like doing it," Ingman said.

I couldn't argue with him about that. Peeling posts helped Dad and it passed the time while I waited for more milk to carry.

But there was one other thing about it, too.

When else could I make a big mess like that and nobody got mad?

✲✲✲✲✲✲✲✲✲✲✲✲✲✲✲✲✲✲✲✲✲

Photo Opportunity

One sunny, Sunday afternoon as I came in the house after checking Dusty's water bucket, I saw my sister's camera sitting on the kitchen table. The camera was shaped like a box, and you held it in front of you and looked down into a square place on the top to see the picture you wanted to take. Loretta always got out her camera at Christmas or Thanksgiving, or when it was someone's birthday. But today was Sunday. It wasn't Christmas, Thanksgiving or anyone's birthday.

I had always thought it would be fun to take pictures with Loretta's camera. It seemed like magic to me that you could press a button, and then, when the film was developed, there was the picture of what you had seen. But so far, I had never gotten the chance to take any pictures. My mother was afraid I would break the camera.

Now—why Mom would think I'd break Loretta's camera was beyond me. It wasn't like I went around breaking things all the time.

Except for the occasional plate, maybe.

Well, okay, one time it was a whole stack of plates. They slipped out of my hands as I was setting the table for supper. The plates were a pale yellow, the color of milk in June when the cows were eating plenty of rich green grass. I was never sure exactly what had happened, but just like that, as I had turned toward the table, the plates slipped out of my hands and went crashing to the floor. Ingman was upstairs trying to sleep because he had to work the night shift at the creamery, and he said it had sounded like a bomb had gone off in the kitchen.

I spent a long time sweeping the kitchen floor to make sure I swept up all the pieces of plates scattered everywhere. Mom said I had to sweep it three times "just to make sure." She did not want anyone to get a piece of plate stuck in a bare foot. I had drawn a breath to say that no one hardly ever went barefoot around the house, but then I had thought better of it and kept my mouth shut.

By then, it was too late to call Loretta at work to tell her to buy some plates on her way home, so Mom had decided we would use the good plates for supper, the dark green ones with the silver maple pattern on them that Loretta had bought for Mom as a gift. I loved the maple leaf plates. They were decorated with the same kind of leaves as the big silver maples that grew around the edge of the yard. We only used the plates at Christmas, Thanksgiving and Easter, so it seemed like an adventure to use them in the middle of the summer for meatloaf and potato salad and sliced tomatoes.

For some reason, though, my mother would not let me get the maple leaf plates out of the buffet in the living room where she kept them. She said she had already lost a perfectly good stack of plates and did not want to lose another set in the same day. We waited until Loretta came home, and then she took out the maple leaf plates and set the table.

My mother would not let me help clear the table, either, after supper was over.

The next day, Loretta had stopped at the dimestore on her way home from work and had bought a kind of plate that was called melamine. Loretta said it was a fancy word for plastic. The plates had big yellow and orange and white flowers on them with green leaves. Mom said the flowers were called chrysanthemums. I thought the plates were pretty. Mom said the plates were pretty, too, but what she really liked about them was I could drop them all I wanted and they wouldn't break.

And then, too, I occasionally dropped a glass and broke it while I was setting the table or clearing the table or drying the dishes. But then, other people broke glasses too. It wasn't just me. One evening I had come in the house while Mom and Loretta were doing the dishes. Dad said he needed another washcloth to wash the cows' udders because the one he was using had started to fall apart. Seconds after the screen door in the porch had slammed shut behind me I had heard the crash of a drinking glass breaking as it dropped onto the floor.

When I had walked in the kitchen, Mom had turned her steely blue eyes in my direction and said she wondered how many thousands of times she would have to tell me not to let the screen door slam behind me before I would remember not to let the screen door slam behind me. "The whole house shakes when you do that. I'm surprised you haven't broken a window yet," she'd said. "And now this. You made your sister nearly jump out of her shoes. That's why she dropped the glass."

"Really?" I said.

"No, no," Loretta said. "It's just that I wasn't expecting the screen door to slam at that moment."

"Oh," I said.

And then, of course, there was the window in the porch door that I had put my hand through while I was hurrying up the steps. I caught my toe, fell forward, and the next thing I knew, my hand had punched through the glass.

My mother was quite upset about the glass in the door because it was a new door. Dad had put it in only a few weeks earlier. He said it would be better than the old screen door because it had a cylinder on it that kept it from slamming shut.

After I put my hand through the glass, Dad said he could see now that it was a poor design and that he should have bought one with glass and a screen in the top instead of in the top and bottom. He said he was glad that I hadn't cut off a finger. Mom said she did not care one bit about my fingers—that she only cared about her new door. Dad got a funny expression on his face, as if he felt a little sick to his stomach. "You don't really mean that," he had said in a low voice.

For only about the second time in my life, I saw my mother look ashamed of herself.

"No," Mom had said with a sigh. "I didn't really mean it."

Dad had gone back to the farm supply store to buy another door with glass and a screen only in the top. I went with him. "Anyone could have tripped on the steps," he said as he was paying for the new door. "Even your mother. Or maybe especially your mother."

As I looked at Loretta's camera sitting on the table, I decided that maybe Mom was right. Maybe I should not be allowed to take a picture with my sister's camera, because to take a picture, I would have to hold the camera, and what if I dropped it and broke it? Or what if I did something else wrong, pushed the wrong button or something?

Just then I heard footsteps coming downstairs. It was my big sister.

"What's the camera for?" I asked.

"I'm going for a walk this afternoon," she said. "Would you like to come with me?"

"A walk where?"

Loretta smiled. "It's such a beautiful day, and I haven't been to the back of the farm in a long time. I want to take some pictures and use up the rest of the film."

As we were talking, Mom made her way out into the kitchen, crutches clicking.

"Did I hear you say you're going for a walk?" she said, setting her crutches against the table.

"Yes," Loretta said.

Mom carefully sat down in her chair. "But," she said, "there's so much snow. How are you going to get back there?"

"I've been thinking about that," Loretta said. "It's been a long time since I've been to the back of the farm. But Dad's been spreading manure yet, hasn't he?"

When the snow became too deep to drive back in the field, Dad would start a manure pile close to the barn. But so far, he was still able to make it back into the field. Dad said he wanted to keep hauling out the manure and spreading it as long as he could because then he wouldn't have so much to haul out in the spring.

"Yes," I said, "Daddy's been hauling manure. With the four-sixty."

Usually my father used the Super C Farmall, his "little tractor," to haul manure. But with so much snow on the ground, he had been using the 460 Farmall, his "big tractor."

"Oh, good," Loretta said. "That means we'll have tractor tracks we can walk in."

"But Loretta," Mom said. "Dad's been hauling *manure*. You don't want to go for a walk out there."

"Sure, why not," Loretta said. "It's a farm, isn't it?"

That was one of the things I found so interesting about my big sister. When she went to work, she wore suits or nice dresses, and jewelry and high heels, and even pretty pink lipstick. She smelled good, too, like flowers. One of the perfumes she liked to wear was called Lily of the Valley. With her dark hair, blue eyes and a smile that made it seem like the day had suddenly gotten more sunshine, she was the prettiest woman I knew. But at home, my sister liked to go for walks around the farm, and sometimes in the summer, she drove the tractor while we were baling hay and also helped unload hay.

"It will be an adventure, won't it," Loretta said, turning to me.

"Well, all right," Mom said. "But whatever you do, don't let your little sister carry the camera. She'll probably break it."

"Mo-om," I said. "I wasn't going to ask to carry the camera."

"That's fine, then," she said.

"The way you make it sound, I break everything I touch."

My mother looked at me steadily. "If the shoe fits, wear it."

"If the shoe fits? What do shoes have to do with anything," I said.

"Oh, never mind," Mom said. "It wasn't that important."

As soon as we came out of the house, Needles strolled out of the granary, wagging his tail and almost turning himself inside-out when my sister reached down to pet him. We climbed over the barnyard fence and made our way to the road Dad used to drive back in the fields. Needles followed along. Like the rest of us, the dog did not get out much for walks during the winter. In the summertime, someone was always outside doing something, so Needles had plenty of company. Nowadays, he spent much of his time in the granary when we were not in the barn.

While we crawled through the gate to get to the road next to the Bluff, Needles crawled under it and then trotted on ahead. Dad had driven back and forth so many times with the tractor that there was plenty of room to walk in the tracks. The bright blue sky arched overhead with not a cloud in sight. Our feet crunched against the tire tracks in the snow, and I could hear a slight breeze rattling the rusty-colored leaves of the oak trees growing on the Bluff. Some of the oaks did not lose their leaves until spring.

My big sister drew in a deep breath and let it out slowly. "Isn't it just gorgeous out here?" she asked. "I'm in the office all week, and sometimes I look out the window and see how nice it is outside, and it just about kills me sometimes."

"The sun is really pretty on the snow," I said.

"And isn't that just about the bluest sky you've ever seen?" Loretta said. "And it's so quiet out here now at this of year, isn't it."

Other than the *crunch-crunch-crunch* sound of our footsteps and the breeze rustling the dry oak leaves, the world was quiet. No birds sang, although a crow *caw-caw-cawed* from the top of one of the trees on the Bluff. Needles trotted on ahead of us, his tail bobbing up and down.

"Do you think Needles gets cold outside at night?" I asked.

"What brought that up?" Loretta replied.

I shrugged and turned to watch my sister's face. She frowned as she thought about what I had said.

"Do *you* think Needles gets cold?" she asked finally.

"I don't know. Dad says *he* would get cold if he had to sleep on a pile of feed sacks in the granary when it's below zero."

"Why doesn't Needles sleep in the barn at night?" Loretta asked.

"He doesn't want to be in there by himself," I said.

"He's not by himself. The cows and the kitties are in the barn."

"That's just it. Some of the cows don't like him, and I think he doesn't want to be there by himself with the cows. That's what Dad thinks too."

"Maybe Daddy should build Needles a dog house and put some insulation in the walls," Loretta said.

"He's already thought of that. But what if Needles won't use it?"

"I don't suppose a dog house would be any warmer than the granary anyway," my sister said.

We walked along without saying anything for a little while. Dad left the gate open at the end of the lane during the winter so he did not have to open and close it every time he drove out with the manure spreader. The tractor tracks went back and forth across the field here, and toward the north side, they went all the way to the stand of big, dark green pine trees at the end of the field.

For a little while, I had almost forgotten why we went for a walk.

"What are you going to take pictures of anyway?" I asked.

Loretta pointed to the rows of pines at the back of the farm. "What about the snow on the trees?"

Toward the end of the week a couple of inches of fluffy snow had fallen that covered the pine trees with white. Later on in the spring when the weather turned warm, snow would not stick to the pine trees very long and would slide off after only a couple of hours in the sun. But today, the trees were still covered in white.

"Looks like a postcard out here, doesn't it?" my sister said.

Now that she mentioned it, the sun sparkling on the snow and the trees covered with white looked exactly like something you'd see on a postcard.

"Or a Christmas card," I said.

"Yes, or a Christmas card," my sister agreed.

For Christmas this year, someone had sent my mother a card with pine trees sketched on the front. The snow on the boughs had been made of silver glitter. When Mom had pulled the card out of the envelope, glitter as fine as dust had clung to her fingers.

As we trudged along the tractor tracks toward the pine trees, Needles continued trotting ahead of us. At any other time, he would have snooped here and there, but because the snow was as deep as he was tall, he had to stay in the tracks.

Eventually the tractor tracks looped around, and we could see where Dad had spread manure on the other side of the field. We had not reached the pines at the back of the farm, although we were right next to the stand of pines that jutted out into the field, planted there to keep a washout from getting worse.

As Loretta began taking pictures of the trees ahead of us, I explored along the edge of the pines next to us. Standing this close to them, I had to tilt my head back to see the top of the trees.

Needles followed in my tracks, and when he reached the fence, he crawled through and made his way over to where there was not as much snow under the pines. Then he happily began sniffing the ground, following his nose here and there. I was surprised to see that there was not more snow on the ground underneath the pine trees, but when I looked up at the trees again, I wondered if it was because so much snow was stuck on the branches that never made it to the ground.

I was so busy watching Needles, and wondering about the snow on the pine boughs, that I did not hear my sister walk up behind me.

"Would you like to take one?" Loretta asked.

I spun around to stare at her.

"What?"

"Do you want to take a picture?"

"A picture? With your camera?"

"Yes, with my camera. What else would you take a picture with?"

"Do you mean it? Could I? Really?"

She smiled and held out the camera.

I started to reach for the Brownie. But all at once I remembered the plates. And the glasses. And the porch door. I put both my hands behind my back and shook my head.

"No, maybe I shouldn't."

"Why not?"

"I might break it."

"What makes you think you'll break it?"

"Don't you remember?" I said.

"Remember what?"

"I broke all those plates that time. And a couple of those glasses Mom got for a Christmas present. And then that one time I let the porch door slam and you dropped a glass. And don't you remember when I broke the window in the porch door? Dad had just put it in and then he had to go and get another one."

My sister shook her head. "Don't be silly. All you've got to do is point it at what you want to take a picture of and then press the button. You won't break it."

I looked at her as the seconds ticked away. Maybe, just maybe, if I was only going to hold the camera and wasn't going to carry it...

"Are you sure it would be all right?" I asked.

"I'm sure. What do you want to take a picture of?" she said.

I turned back toward the trees and saw the way the sun slanted along the tree trunks and lit up the ground underneath.

"Could I take a picture of that?" I asked, pointing.

"Of what?"

"The way the sun is shining through the trees," I explained.

Loretta reached up with one hand to pull her hat down over her ears a little more.

"Well, ummm...I don't know if that will work." She glanced at the camera. "And we've only got one picture left."

Needles, who had been snooping back and forth and here and there, saw us standing by the fence and started toward us.

"That's okay," I said. "If you've only got one picture left, maybe I shouldn't."

"Well, I guess there's only one way to find out if it *will* work," Loretta continued. "I just hope you won't be disappointed if it doesn't turn out. I've never taken a picture like that before, so I don't know how it will work."

Loretta handed the camera to me. "Hold it in front of you and look down into that little square glass on the top. What do you see?"

"The trees and the sun shining through them," I said.

"Okay. When the camera is where you want it pointed, push the button down."

I spent a long minute or two trying to decide if I had the camera pointed where I wanted it. Finally I pushed down the button.

"You did it!" Loretta said. "You took a picture!"

I carefully handed the camera back to my sister. Now that I had taken the picture, I could feel my hands starting to tremble. If I dropped the camera and broke it, I knew I would never hear the end of it from my mother.

"Well, I don't know about you," Loretta said, "but my feet are starting to get a little cold."

Now that she mentioned it, my feet felt a little tingly, too.

"Come on Needles," I said.

The dog followed in our footprints until we reached Dad's tractor tire tracks, and then he trotted in front of us once again.

A little while later, we arrived back at the house.

"Did you have a nice walk?" Mom called out from the living room. She was sitting in her chair by the picture window.

"Lovely," Loretta said. "It looks just like a postcard outside."

Loretta and I went into the living room and sat down on the davenport.

"You didn't break the camera, did you?" Mom said.

"No. I didn't break the camera," I said.

"She didn't break your camera, did she?" Mom asked.

Loretta shook her head. "What would make you think she'd break my camera?"

"I know how she is," Mom said. "She pesters about everything, and I figured once you got out there, she'd pester you to let her take a picture."

"Nope. She did not pester me to let her take a picture," Loretta said.

"Good," Mom said.

"I told her to take a picture."

"You did *what*?" my mother asked.

"I told her to take a picture. She didn't want to because she was afraid she'd break the camera. But there was only one picture left, and I want to get the film developed."

"Are you *sure* you didn't drop it?" Mom said to me.

"I did *not* drop it," I said.

"She did not even come *close* to dropping it," Loretta said.

My mother sighed. "Well, all right. I guess there's no harm done."

Later in the afternoon, Loretta gathered her things together so she could drive back to her apartment for the week.

"I will take the film in tomorrow, and it ought to be developed by Friday," she said. "When I come home next weekend, then we can see what our pictures look like."

The weeks always seemed long during the winter while Loretta was staying at her apartment. But this week seemed especially long, more like a month rather than a week.

Finally Friday arrived. I went out to the barn to help Dad feed the cows before supper, and I practically trotted along, pushing the big push broom as fast as I could to sweep out the mangers.

"What are you in such a hurry for?" Dad asked.

"Loretta's coming home soon," I said.

"She usually does on Friday night," Dad said.

"She was going to get the film developed this week."

"Film?" Dad said.

"From our walk last Sunday. She let me take a picture!"

"She did?" Dad said.

"She said it probably wouldn't turn out. But even if it doesn't, I want to see the pictures she took," I said.

I was watching out the south barn window, and my father had started to climb down the haymow ladder after throwing hay down for the cows, when I saw headlights coming over the hill by the church.

"Loretta's here!" I said.

"You'd better go to the house then," Dad said.

"Don't you want me to help feed hay?"

Dad shook his head. "I think I can manage all by myself for once."

I had reached the corner of the garage when Loretta drove up the hill of our driveway. She parked the car and got out.

"Did you get the pictures?" I asked.

"Yes, I got the pictures," she said.

My sister went into the house. I stopped in the porch to take off my boots and my chore coat. When I opened the kitchen door, Loretta was already showing the pictures to Mom.

"And look at this," she said. "This is the prettiest one of all."

I peeked over my sister's shoulder.

It was a picture of the sun shining through the pine trees.

"But," I said, "but ... that's the one I took!"

"It is," Loretta said. "And isn't it pretty."

The picture showed the sun slanting along the tree trunks, and as I looked at it, I could remember the way I had felt, standing by the fence, getting ready to take the picture.

"See?" Loretta said. "And you were worried you'd break the camera."

Of course I was worried.

There were only so many hours in the day. It had taken me a very long time doing extra chores around the house such as washing windows and cleaning out closets to work off paying for the plates and the glasses. Not to mention the new door.

I did not even want to *think* about paying for a camera.

****

~ 15 ~
Nuggersprit

As the bus chugged down the last hill on the way to our farm, sledding was the farthest thing from my mind. Even though the sun had been shining all day, the weather had remained cold, and right before lunch, our teacher had told us we could stay inside at recess if we wanted to.

I had ventured outside along with a couple of other kids from my class. But after a few minutes, our eyes began to water because the air was so cold, and we had decided to go back inside. No one went outside during afternoon recess. It was the first time since we had been back at school after Christmas vacation that the weather was so cold we could stay inside during recess if we wanted to.

The bus driver pulled into the driveway and waited until I stood by the steps to open the door. "It's too cold to leave the door open for very long," he said. In the spring and the fall, the bus driver would push the lever for the door as soon as he stopped in the driveway.

I made my way down the steps, jumped off the last big step—and that's when I started thinking about my sled.

The snow beneath my feet was so smooth and polished that I slid forward without hardly even trying. In the good old days, before Mom started worrying about cars on the road and said if I wanted to slide at all, I had to use the pasture, I would wait for perfect conditions just like this.

As I started up the driveway, a thought that I did not want to think, that I knew I should not think, kept trying to push its way into the front of my mind. After a while, I could not ignore it anymore: I really, really, *really* wanted to take my sled down the driveway. Smooth, packed snow like this only came along a couple of times during the winter.

Maybe, if I asked in just the right way, I could talk Mom into letting me slide down a couple of times. After all, it wouldn't hurt to ask. Even though I was pretty sure she would say no.

I hurried the rest of the way up the hill and into the house. My mother was sitting by the kitchen table, peeling potatoes.

"You're out of breath. What are you in such a hurry for?" Mom said.

I had been trying to decide the best to way ask and figured, since it would not be long until dark, that I ought to just come right out with it.

"Would it be all right," I said, "if I took my sled down the driveway a couple of times?"

"Isn't it kind of cold out for that?" Mom asked, selecting another potato to peel.

"Please? Please-please-please?" I said. "I'll only go a couple of times."

I went into the small hallway by the kitchen to hang my coat up in the closet.

"Please? Please-please-please?" I said, as I turned back toward the kitchen.

"You know how I feel about you sliding down the driveway. It's dangerous," Mom said.

My sense of anticipation began to fade. "Yes, I know," I said.

"What if a car comes along right when you reach the bottom of the hill?" she asked.

I didn't think it would do any good to explain, yet again, that the only cars that drove on our road were the school bus, the milk truck, Dad coming home from the feed mill, my sister coming home from work Friday night or my brother coming home from the creamery.

My mother stopped peeling the potato and looked at me for what seemed like a very long time.

"Do you promise," she said at last, "not to start down the hill if you hear a car coming?"

My sense of anticipation returned. "Yes! I promise!"

"And do you promise to only go down a couple of times? It will be getting dark soon."

"Yes! I promise!"

"Well, I suppose. Just this once."

I could hardly believe what I was hearing.

My mother held up her hand. "But don't hug me. I'm trying to get these potatoes peeled."

"Yes, Mom," I said.

"Now hurry up if you're going."

Usually I ate a snack as soon as I got home from school.

Today I forgot all about eating a snack and raced upstairs to change my clothes. A few minutes later I had put on my coat and boots and was ready to head out the door.

"Just remember: only a couple of times," Mom said.

"I'll remember."

I trotted out to the machine shed to grab my sled from where it leaned against the wall next to my toboggan.

A minute later, I was racing down the hill.

When I reached the bottom of the driveway, my sled was already slowing down, but it still went almost to the other side of the road.

I stood up, grabbed the twine string Dad had braided into a rope and pulled my sled back up the hill.

The second trip was every bit as good as the first.

After I had gone down the driveway the fourth time, I knew Mom would be upset if I went down again because by now it was nearly dark.

I headed back to the machine shed with my sled, and to tell the truth, I didn't mind putting my sled away. My feet were starting to feel so cold it was hard to tell where my toes ended and my winter boots began. I should have put on an extra pair of socks before I left the house, but I had been in such a hurry to go sliding, I forgot all about putting on more socks.

By the time I reached the machine shed, walking still felt strange. I knew I was walking because I was moving, but I could not feel the ground beneath my feet. I put my sled away in the machine shed and then I headed for the house.

I did not even stop in the porch to take off my boots. When I opened the house door, the kitchen was filled with the smell of boiling potatoes, and steam puffed out from beneath the lid of the kettle in which my mother always cooked potatoes.

I hung my coat up on the newel post and set my hat and mittens on the steps. Then I moved over to Dad's chair and sat down so I could take off my boots.

"What's wrong with your feet? Why are you walking that way?" Mom said.

"What way?" I said. I pulled off one boot and leaned over to set it by the furnace grate in the corner.

"You're walking like you don't know where your feet are," she said.

"I can't feel my feet," I said, pulling off the other boot.

"What was that?"

"I can't feel my feet," I said.

"Take your socks off," Mom said.

"My socks?"

"I want to see your feet."

I pulled off one sock and then the other.

"Come over here," Mom said.

Whenever I could, I avoided walking barefoot on the kitchen linoleum in the winter. But since my feet were so cold, I did not notice that the floor was cold.

My mother stared down at my feet. "They're a little white. Maybe you'd better sit by the furnace until they warm up."

The furnace itself was right below the floor beneath the square grate in the corner. If I stood next to the furnace grate when Mom turned up the thermostat on the wall by the kitchen sink, I could see little blue flames down inside the furnace.

My mother pushed herself up from her chair and inched around until she could grab hold of the edge of the countertop with one hand. Shuffling sideways, she moved over until she had reached the thermostat.

"I'm going to turn the furnace up," she said. "That will help your feet get warm faster."

I turned Dad's chair around, put my feet flat on the floor and pushed them closer to the grate. I leaned forward a little, and sure enough, I could see small blue flames deep inside the furnace.

In no time at all, the floor around the grate was as warm as the concrete porch steps on a hot summer day. As I sat there letting my feet warm up, I huddled closer to the heat coming up from the furnace, it seemed to me that if I closed my eyes, I could go right to sleep sitting in the chair.

All at once, I stopped feeling sleepy. I looked down at my feet. Instead of white, they were bright red. And they no longer felt numb. They felt like they were on fire.

"Ouch!" I said, pushing Dad's chair back.

"What's wrong," Mom said. She had moved over to the stove and stood poised with a fork in her hand so she could check the potatoes.

"My feet were numb before. But now they feel like they're on fire."

My mother smiled. "You have nuggersprit," she said.

The word sounded like a cross between a cough and a sneeze.

"I have nug-what?" I said.

"Nuggersprit."

"What's nugger—?"

"Sprit. That's what it's called it when you frostbite your feet or your hands, and then when they start to get warm, they feel like they're burning up."

"Frostbite!" I exclaimed. My stomach performed a small flip-flop at the very thought. I had read about frostbite in one of the books at school and how people sometimes lost their fingers and toes afterward. It sounded terrible—the skin turned all black and bruised.

I looked down at my feet again. I did not want to lose my toes.

"Well," Mom said, "you probably didn't actually get frostbite. Your feet were white, but they didn't look like white paper. And they weren't waxy. I wouldn't worry about it."

"But they hurt!"

My mother wasn't smiling anymore. "I know. Walk around a little bit. That will help the stingy-feeling to go away."

"Walk around? But my feet hurt!" I said.

"I know. It doesn't sound like much fun. But it will help."

I stood up and took a few steps toward the kitchen sink. My toes felt like they wanted to break off from my feet.

"Ouch, ouch, ouch," I said.

"It will get better," Mom said.

I turned and walked back toward Dad's chair and then behind the table.

My toes still felt like they were going break off.

"Keep going," Mom said.

After a few trips around the table, my feet started to feel a little better, although they still looked sort of red. I put my socks back on and went upstairs to get the pink fuzzy slippers Loretta had given to me for Christmas.

"Where did that word come from anyway?" I asked, as I took the plates from the cupboard so I could set the table. "It's sounds so funny."

"It's a Norwegian word. At least I think it's Norwegian. That's what my mother and father always called it."

"Did you get nugger...nugger..."

"Sprit," my mother supplied.

"Did you get nuggersprit when you were little, too?"

My mother smiled and pushed back a lock of her dark curly hair. "Oh, boy, did I. Especially my toes. You really wouldn't think that something like your feet warming up again could hurt so much, would you."

A few minutes later, Dad came in from the barn for supper.

"What happened to you kiddo? Usually you come out to the barn to help me," he said. He hung his cap over my coat on the newel post.

"Her feet got cold," Mom said.

"Just from walking up from the bus?" Dad asked.

"No. She went sledding for a little while on the driveway," Mom said.

"On the *driveway*?" Dad asked. "I thought you didn't want her to slide on the driveway."

"I don't. Not really. But she's a little older now. And I made her promise to watch for cars before she started down," Mom said.

"Oh, I see," Dad said.

"And then she got nuggersprit," Mom said.

"That's bad," my father said.

"Have you ever gotten nuggersprit?" I asked.

Dad shook his head. "I can't get nuggersprit."

"You can't?" I said.

"Nope. I'm not Norwegian. That's only for Norwegian people."

"Roy," my mother said. "Don't be silly. Everyone can get nuggersprit."

My father's mother had come from Germany and his father had come from Scotland.

Dad grinned and threw another wink in my direction. "Yes, my feet have gotten that cold. I try not to let it happen, though, if I can help it," he said, heading toward the bathroom so he could wash his hands before supper.

The next day at school, the weather was not quite as cold, and we all went outside for noon recess. The teacher said we should go outside for some fresh air but that we could come in early if we started to feel cold, just as long as we did not make a mess in the classroom.

When we came back inside, one girl said her feet were so cold she could not feel them. The teacher told her to take her boots off, sit on the counter and put her feet on the heat register.

Now here was something new. None of our teachers had ever told us we could sit on the counter.

A few minutes later, the girl took her feet off the heat register and began pulling off her socks. "Ouch!" she said. "My feet were cold. But now they hurt. And look how red they are!"

The teacher came over to look at the girl's feet. So did many of my classmates, me included.

"You have nuggersprit," I said.

"I have what?"

"Nuggersprit."

"What kind of a word is that?"

"It's Norwegian," I said. "It's what they call it when your feet hurt when they start to warm up again."

"I'm not Norwegian," the girl said. "My mom says we're German and Irish."

"Everyone can get nuggersprit," I said.

"What did you say that word was?" the teacher asked.

"Nuggersprit," I said.

The teacher shook her head. "Never heard of it. I'll have to try to remember it, though. It's a good word. How is it spelled?"

I had never asked Mom how it was spelled.

"I don't know," I said.

"Well, never mind. I think I can remember it anyway," the teacher said. "It must have something to do with frostbite."

"Frostbite!" said the girl who had been sitting with her feet on the heat register. "I don't want frostbite."

"Put your shoes back on and walk around for a little bit. That will probably help," the teacher said.

"My feet are cold, too," said one of the boys.

"So are mine."

"Mine, too."

"Can we sit with our feet on the register to see if we get that funny word?" one of the girls asked.

The teacher looked at us. "There's not enough room on the countertop for everyone."

"We can sit in our chairs and put our feet up. See? Like this," said one of the boys as he demonstrated putting his feet on the register.

The teacher sighed and looked at the clock. "You have precisely seven minutes. I want everyone back at their desks in seven minutes. Then we have to start Social Studies."

The clattering and scraping of chairs filled the room, and when it quieted down, a dozen kids were sitting next to the heat register.

As it turned out, no one else got nuggersprit that day. Some of the boys were disappointed, too, because they wanted to see what it felt like.

I already knew what it felt like, though. I'd had it once.

And let me tell you—once was more than enough.

****

Cockleburs, Sandpaper and Toothpicks...

Although it was something I did every day, I still would rather not put on clean clothes during the winter. If I took a pair of socks out of the drawer and slid them over my feet, suddenly, it felt as if someone had lined my socks with cockleburs.

If I put on a clean pair of pants, whoever had put the cockleburs in my socks had apparently also lined my pant legs with sandpaper.

If I pulled on a clean sweatshirt, the person responsible for the cockleburs and the sandpaper must have also put toothpicks inside my sweatshirt.

Complaining to my mother didn't help, though.

"I'm sorry," Mom said one afternoon as I tried to get at my back from one side and then the other. "But it's because I have to dry the clothes in the basement."

I had just put on my clean, red sweatshirt. It was my favorite sweatshirt. Except that right now, there was a particular spot on my back that prickled and itched. But I couldn't reach it.

"What does drying the clothes in the basement have to do with it?" I asked as I twisted the other way, trying to reach the itchy spot on my back.

Downstairs in the basement was a wringer washer that Mom used to wash clothes. Mom said she really liked the wringer washer because she could let Dad's work clothes wash for as long as it took to get them clean. During the summer, our clothes hung outside to dry, but in the winter, they hung in the basement.

"There's no wind in the basement," replied Dad. He was sitting by the kitchen table with a cup of coffee and a stack of Loretta's peanut butter cookies. My sister usually baked a couple of batches of cookies when she was home on the weekend.

"What does wind have to do with it?" I asked.

"During the summer, when the clothes are dried outside, the wind fluffs them up. But now this time of year, when they're in the basement, there's nothing to move 'em around."

"I suppose it doesn't help that I use starch, either," Mom said.

From what I knew about starch, it was supposed to make the clothes stiff.

"Why do you need to use starch?" I asked.

"It helps the wrinkles come out when I iron," she explained.

To be completely honest, it wouldn't matter to me one bit if my clothes were wrinkled. But not only did Mom iron my sweatshirts, she also ironed the sheets and the pillowcases. And the dishtowels. And the dishcloths. And even the bath towels and the washcloths.

When I spoke up and said it would not matter to me if my clothes were wrinkled, Mom looked shocked.

"I'm not going to allow my family to walk around in wrinkled clothes," she said.

Dad took a sip of coffee and set his cup back down on the table. "Maybe one of those new clothes dryers would help," he said. "Maybe, with a dryer, you wouldn't have to iron everything."

"What's a clothes dryer?" I asked.

"Just what it sounds like," Mom said.

"It's a machine that dries the clothes," Dad explained. "They've got 'em advertised in the newspaper here." He opened the newspaper and pointed to something that looked like a big square box.

"How does it work?" I asked.

"It's got a drum inside," he said.

"Like the drums they play in a band?"

He shook his head. "Like a barrel. You put the clothes in and it goes around and heats up. It would fluff the clothes like the wind does outside in the summer," Dad said.

A glimmer of hope flickered in the back of my mind.

"Can we get one?" I asked, turning toward my mother.

She shook her head. "No, we cannot."

"But why not?"

"Too expensive," Mom said. "I don't have the money to buy a clothes dryer. And besides, our electric bills are high enough as it is. It costs a lot of money, you know, to keep that milkhouse heater going so the pipes don't freeze."

The glimmer of hope disappeared. "Oh," I said, looking at Dad.

He shrugged apologetically as he reached for another cookie.

"Say—before you put on something clean, maybe you could try shaking it out," Dad suggested, breaking the cookie in half so he could dunk it in his coffee.

My mother nodded. "That might work. You know, like you shake a rug."

"You wouldn't be able to shake them as long as the wind does when the clothes are out on the line, but it might help," Dad said.

The next morning before I got dressed to go out to the barn, I came downstairs with an armful of clothes. The night before when I had fed the calves, one of them had flipped the calf bucket out of the manger and had splashed milk all over my pants. I had put the pants in the hamper when I came in from the barn, so now I needed a clean pair of chore pants. I knew the clean pants were going to feel scratchy and prickly. But my favorite red sweatshirt was still prickly, too.

I figured I might as well try shaking out both the clean pants and the sweatshirt before I put them on.

"Where are you going?" Mom inquired. As she usually was most mornings, my mother was sitting by the table with a cup of coffee.

"I'm going outside to shake my clothes," I said.

My mother frowned. "Not in your pajamas and slippers. It's winter."

I turned to look at her. "You mean I have to get dressed just to go outside and shake these?"

"What does the thermometer say?" Mom asked.

I set my armful of clothes on the steps and went over the kitchen window by the furnace grate.

"It's…"

I leaned closer so I could see better.

"It's ten below zero," I said.

"Ten below!" Mom said.

She paused. "Well, I suppose you won't be out there that long. But at least put on a coat and boots. And some mittens. And maybe your stocking cap."

If I had to put on my coat, boots, mittens and stocking cap, I might just as well get dressed and forget about shaking out my clothes.

On the other hand, if I did not shake out my clothes, I would never know if it would help.

A minute later, I stood on the step, shivering and feeling slightly silly, wearing a coat over my pajamas. Because it had been hanging in the porch, my coat made me feel like I was wrapped in ice cubes. My boots, which had been sitting in the porch, too, were not any better.

I laid the sweatshirt across the porch railing and took hold of the pants by the waistband. From the other side of the garage, I heard a wheezy *chuff-chuff-chuff-chuff* as the milker pump started up. If Dad had already started the milker pump, that meant it would not be long before there was milk to carry.

I took hold of my pants by the waistband. Or at least I tried to.

Hanging onto a pair of pants by the waistband with mittens on my hands was not the easiest thing in the world. Before I could get a better grip on them, the pants slid out of my grip and landed in the snow beside the porch.

Great. Now my pants were full of snow.

I clomped down the steps and stepped into the snow beside the porch. The snow was deep enough that it went over the top of my boots, and I could feel some of it filtering down into my socks. I heaved a deep sigh, reached for my pants, backed out of the snow and clomped back up the steps.

Maybe if I could get my thumbs through the belt loops, I would be able to hang onto them better.

It only took a few seconds for me to figure out that slipping my thumbs through the belt loops while wearing mittens wasn't going to be that easy. Fitting my left thumb into the belt loop was not too difficult because I could use my right hand to help. But once my left thumb was through the loop, I had to use the fingers of my left hand, with the mitten over them, to try to slip my right thumb through the loop.

In the meantime, the cold air continued seeping through the thin fabric of my pajama bottoms, and I could feel my legs turning numb with cold.

At last I managed to get both of my thumbs through the belt loops.

Whenever I helped my big sister clean the living room, Mom said I had to give the rugs twenty-five "good shakes." "Don't just wave them around. Shake them hard enough so they snap," she instructed me every time I headed out the door with a rug to shake.

Twenty-five good shakes took a long time, and I usually needed a couple of breaks. But, if it was good enough for the living room rugs, it ought to be good enough for my clothes.

Shaking the rugs hard enough so they made a snapping noise was not nearly so hard as shaking out my pants. With grim determination, I held onto the belt loops and went to work. Once I had completed the twenty-five, I gave them an extra five shakes just for good measure.

If it seemed to me that getting my thumbs through the belt loops had been just about impossible, removing my thumbs was every bit as difficult.

When my thumbs were finally free of the belt loops, I hung the pants over the railing and picked up my red sweatshirt. By now I was not shivering anymore, but when I stopped at ten shakes to give my arms a rest, the sweatshirt slipped from my grasp. It, too, landed in the snow.

Once again I clomped down the steps. This time I could use my footprints from the time before. I waded into the snow by the porch, grabbed my sweatshirt, and backed out of the snow. I clomped up the porch steps and gave the sweatshirt another fifteen shakes.

Feeling like my legs would never be warm again, I draped the sweatshirt over my arm, picked up the pants and went into the porch. I stood for a moment, trying to decide if I should take my boots off or wear them into the house. I would be going out to the barn as soon as I got dressed, so I might as well wear my boots into the house where they could sit by the furnace grate until I was ready to go outside.

"You were out there an awfully long time. What happened?" Mom asked.

I laid my clothes across a kitchen chair and sat down to take off my boots.

"I dropped my pants in the snow," I said, setting my boots by the furnace.

"Oh, no," Mom said.

"Then I dropped my sweatshirt in the snow."

My mother quickly put her hand up to her mouth, and I knew that she was trying not to smile. She cleared her throat. "I hope you were able to shake all the snow out of them," she said.

"Me, too," I said.

I picked up my sweatshirt and pants and headed upstairs. My feet felt damp from the snow that had filtered into my boots, so I decided I might as well change my socks while I was at it.

The dry socks, since they were in my dresser drawer upstairs, only felt slightly cold, no more so than any of my other clothes upstairs.

But the pants and the sweatshirt—well, the pants and sweatshirt were a different story.

At first, I couldn't tell if shaking out my clothes had helped because the cloth felt so cold against my skin.

Unfortunately, about the same time my clothes warmed up, I noticed that the prickly feeling was still there.

Well, at least I could say one thing—instead of being half asleep when I got ready to go out to the barn, I was wide awake.

Definitely wide awake.

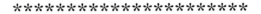

~ 17 ~
The Coldest Day of the Year

One Saturday toward the end of January, right at noon, the thermometer still read minus fifteen degrees. "Seems like this weather just doesn't want to let up," Dad said as he speared a piece of Swiss steak with his fork and passed the plate to me. The kitchen was filled with the mouth-watering aroma of steak and onions, cooked carrots and fresh-baked bread. Mom, Dad, Loretta and I were eating dinner. Ingman was working at the creamery.

"It's only been a few days, but when it's this cold, every day seems like a week," Dad continued.

"Yes, I suppose it is kind of cold out," Mom said. She buttered a slice of bread still warm from the oven and bit into it.

Loretta spooned candied carrots onto her plate and handed the bowl to me. "I wonder if there will be church tomorrow?"

"Probably not," Dad replied. "It's hard to heat the church in weather like this."

I knew that when it was cold outside, it was a good idea to keep my coat on in our little white country church.

My father laid down his fork and looked at Mom. "Do you still want to go to town this afternoon?" He reached for his coffee cup and sipped carefully at the hot liquid, waiting for her to answer.

"Oh, yes. We need groceries," Mom said. "I wish we could have gone earlier in the week."

"Me, too," Dad said. "It was warmer then. But I had to fix the barn cleaner that one day. And then the manure spreader chain broke. And I had to grind feed."

My mother sighed. "Seemed like it was always something."

"That's farming," Dad replied.

"I know," Mom said.

"Could you wait to go to town until the weather warms up a little bit? Maybe it will during the week," Dad said.

My mother shook her head. "I suppose I *could* wait. But I don't want to. We're almost out of flour, and sugar, too. And yeast. I can't bake bread without yeast."

"Okay," Dad said. "We'll go today then."

My father picked up his fork again. "Say kiddo, pass me the salt shaker, will you?"

The salt and pepper shakers were copper and matched the canisters on the counter top. I handed the salt shaker to Dad.

As he reached for the shaker, I was surprised to see his right eye close in a quick wink.

"This is the coldest day we've had so far this year. If the car didn't have a good heater," Dad said as he sprinkled salt on his food, "I wouldn't suggest going to town."

My mother turned to look at me. "You're coming to town with us, you know. You need new mittens and boots."

"Why do I need mittens and boots? I already have mittens and boots," I said.

Mom fixed me with her stern, steel-blue eyes. "You need new mittens and boots. Your old mittens are just about worn out. And I think those boots are too tight on you now. There's no room for any extra socks if you need them."

"It's warm in the bus," I pointed out. "And they don't make us go outside for recess when it's really cold."

I had gotten the boots I wore for school last winter. Seeing as they had been a size too big, Mom said she'd hoped they would last for two winters. I did not want to go to town with Mom and Dad if I could help it because shopping was no fun at all. But if I stayed home—and so did Loretta—maybe I could talk her into baking a batch of chocolate chip cookies.

"You're coming with us, and that's that," Mom said. She turned to my sister. "What are you going to do this afternoon?"

"Hmmmmm," Loretta said, fluffing her curly, dark hair, "I think I'll just stay here and get some cleaning done."

I stared at my big sister. Cleaning? That did not sound like much fun, either. When Loretta cleaned, she went all out. Moving furniture. Vacuuming. Dusting. Shaking rugs.

Maybe going to town with Mom and Dad wouldn't be so bad, at that.

Right after dinner, Mom, Dad and I set off for town. I hurried out to the car, not wanting to spend any more time than necessary in air that was so cold my nostrils pinched shut when I took a deep breath. Dad had started the car a while ago so it would be warm by the time my mother got there. I felt bad about getting into the car while Mom was still walking from the house, but I knew if I got out of the car to keep her company on her slow journey, she would tell me to go and get into the car.

When Mom had almost reached the car, Dad leaned over to trip the latch and pushed the door open a few inches. That way, she only had to pull the door open and did not have to spend time fumbling with her crutches and the door latch.

"Brrrrr!" Mom said as she put her crutches into the car. "You weren't kidding that the wind is cold. And it's not even very windy!"

While my mother went about the business of getting herself settled, I twisted around in the back seat, looking this way and that for Needles. On a cold day like this, I thought he might be curled up on the south side of the garage where he was in the sun and out of the wind.

But I could not see Needles anywhere.

"Where's Needles, Daddy?" I asked.

"Probably in the granary," he replied. "When the door's open this time of day the sun shines right in on his feed sacks."

Instead of backing up, Dad drove around by the machine shed. "See?" he said.

Sure enough, the granary door was wide open. I settled back against the seat as we headed down the driveway, happy to know the dog's feed sacks were in the sun. Sometimes during the winter, I liked sprawling out, too, on the living room floor in the patch of sunshine coming through the window.

But then I had another thought. The granary door and the living room window faced the same direction, and I knew the sun did not shine into the living room for very long at this time of year. What would Needles do for the rest of the afternoon when the sun had moved beyond the granary door?

My mother firmly believed dogs belonged outside. Needles had come to live with us a couple of years ago during the summer when he was a tiny puppy. Loretta had been hanging clothes outside on the clothesline. She was wearing shorts and sandals. When the puppy nipped her ankles, she said, "Get those needles out of here!" And the name had stuck.

From the very beginning, Mom had said many times that she did not want Needles to think he could stay in the house. During the summer, she let him come in the house sometimes when it was going to storm because the dog was afraid of storms. One time he had even been inside all day because he knew it was going to storm. He had stayed close to Mom, and Dad had said he was trying to protect her. And sometimes Needles would come in with Dad at breakfast, dinner or supper, although Mom always insisted that he go right back outside again when Dad went outside. But once the weather turned colder, Mom would not let him come in the house at all. She said it was bad enough that she was cooped up in the house during cold weather, never mind being cooped up with a dog.

Even with the heater going full blast, the car never warmed up completely, and by the time we arrived in town, my toes and fingers felt cold in spite of my boots and mittens. My nose was cold, too, and for once I did not mind strolling up and down the grocery aisles because it was warm inside the store.

"Feels a lot better in here doesn't it," my mother said. She grasped the handle of the grocery cart with both hands. Her crutches dangled from her forearms and sometimes clanked against the wire basket. The crutches were made of metal and had a wide metal cuff, like a bracelet open on one side, that fit over her forearms. The grips she held onto were covered with gray rubber, like the rubber tips at the bottom. When I was a very little girl, my mother had used a pair of wooden crutches with leather strings at the top that fit over her arms.

Mom slowly walked along the grocery store aisle, pushing the cart. When she saw something she needed, she either asked me to get it or she would let go of the cart and put her arms down by her sides until the crutches touched the floor. Then she would make her way over to the shelf, pick out what she wanted, and would hand it to me to put in the cart.

If I had stayed at home, then Dad would have to put things in the cart for my mother. Today, he trailed along behind us, making helpful suggestions from time to time. "Do we need more molasses?" "Have we got enough brown sugar?' "What about some salt? The last time I filled the salt shaker, the box didn't have very much in it."

When we were finished with the groceries, we went to another store to shop for mittens and boots. The ordeal was not nearly as terrible as I had feared. I found a pair of fleecy, bright blue mittens with white cuffs and a white winter hat that tied in front with long strings and had pom-poms on the ends. The hat looked like it was made of fur but it wasn't really fur. And when Mom insisted I try on short boots with fleece around the top that were just like my old ones—Dad pointed out a pair of tall, black boots he said would be better because I wouldn't get snow down inside them when I played outside at recess.

The black, fleece-lined boots were a little big but Mom said that was all right because then I could wear extra socks. She also said she was not going to make the same mistake twice of thinking boots could last me for two years.

The drive home did not seem nearly as long as the drive into town, and before I knew it, Dad turned off the road and headed up our driveway. The sun was already hanging low in the sky.

"Come on, kiddo, let's carry the groceries inside," Dad said, opening the trunk of the car.

"Remember," Mom said, as she got out of the car, "to come back for more." She pulled out her crutches and fitted her arms into the metal cuffs.

"Yes, Mom," I said, heading toward the house with a bag of groceries.

When I got inside the kitchen, I set down the groceries and went back to the porch to hold the door open for Dad. He had a bag in each arm and one clasped between his fingers. The black leather gloves he wore made his hands look bigger and more square than they usually did.

As I held the door for Dad, I looked around, glancing first beside the porch and then over by the car. Something was missing.

"Where's Needles, Daddy?"

Dad stopped and looked around, too.

"Don't know," he said. "Usually he's right out here when we come home, isn't he."

My father took a firmer grip on the grocery bags. "Maybe Needles is still sleeping in the granary and didn't hear us," he said.

I went into the porch to open the house door for him. "Should I go look for Needles?" I asked.

"If you want," Dad replied over his shoulder before stepping into the house.

I leaped down the steps and trotted past Mom. The air was still cold enough to make my nostrils pinch shut, but I didn't care. I was too worried about Needles.

"Where are you going in such a hurry?" my mother asked. She leaned heavily on her crutches, peering sharply at the frozen, white path Dad had shoveled. She was always on the alert for icy patches.

"I'm going to the granary to look for Needles," I said.

I trotted past the garage and the machine shed. The air had felt cold before, but now that the sun was starting to set, it had taken on an even sharper edge. I climbed the granary steps and looked inside.

Needles was nowhere to be seen.

I trotted back to the car just as Dad took the last paper bag of groceries from the trunk.

"Daddy! Needles isn't in the granary."

"He's not?"

"No," I said. "So where is he?"

"Good question," Dad replied. "It's too cold for him to be wandering around outside. In this kind of weather, it wouldn't take long to freeze his ears. We'll get this stuff in the house. Then maybe we should look for him."

I had never thought about Needles freezing his ears.

"Could Needles *really* freeze his ears?"

My father nodded. "The cats could, too. And the cows. But they're all in the barn."

"What about Dusty?" I asked. I knew she couldn't freeze her ears now because the pony had been in the barn since last night. But still.

Dad laughed. "Dusty? Freeze her ears? With all that hair?"

I could see Dad's point. Dusty had just as much hair on her ears as she did everywhere else.

Inside the kitchen, warm air blew out of the furnace grate, and in the living room, a fire crackled in the wood stove. The table was covered with paper bags of groceries, and through the living room doorway I could see Loretta, wearing a blue bandanna over her hair and with a dust cloth in her hand, wiping down the top of the sewing machine. She turned and waved the dust cloth at me. "Did you get boots?"

"Yes, tall black ones!" I replied. Even from the kitchen, I could smell the oily, bitter odor of the spray Loretta had used on the dust cloth.

My sister smiled. "Can I see them?"

I grabbed my new boots and took them into the living room. As I walked through the door, I glimpsed a patch of white on the davenport to my left. Holding out the boots toward Loretta, I turned to look at the white thing.

It was Needles.

"What —!"

"Shhhh," Loretta whispered, holding her finger up to her lips. She tilted her head toward the kitchen where Mom had started to put away the groceries, the bags rustling and crackling as she reached inside them.

I clapped my hand over my mouth and stared at Needles, feeling a giggle bubbling up in my chest. The dog faced the room, paws and nose over the edge of the seat, bright eyes watching me, ears perked. He flipped his tail up and down against the cushions, which had been covered with clean, white rag rugs.

The white rugs had not been on the davenport this morning.

"Come on, kiddo," Dad said, walking into the living room. "We have to go look for Nee—" He glanced at the davenport and stopped short. "Whaaa —"

"Shhhhh," Loretta and I cautioned, fingers over our lips.

"All right," Mom said from the kitchen. "What's going on in there? That's the second 'shhh' I've heard in the last two minutes."

"Nothing's going on," Loretta replied.

"I'm a mother," Mom said, hanging onto the edge of the stove and peering through the doorway at us. "I know when something is going on." She grabbed hold of the doorjamb, came into the living room and glanced at the davenport.

She started to say something but then turned to look at the davenport again.

"What," she said, "is that dog doing in here, if I may ask?"

Loretta sighed. "Mother, it's so cold. I went out to shake some rugs and I practically froze stiff in the minute I was out there, and then Needles came out of the granary. Usually he trots around when he's outside, but today, he just sort of crept up to me, all hunched together like he was trying to stay warm. He looked at me with those big, brown eyes. And then he started shivering. I just couldn't stand the thought of him being outside another minute. I'm worried he'll freeze his ears. Or his feet. Or that he'll get sick."

Meanwhile, Needles remained on the davenport, nose and paws hanging over the edge. He rolled his eyes in Mom's direction.

"Just look at him," Loretta said.

"I am," my mother replied grimly. "He's on my davenport, of all places."

"Yes — " Loretta said, "but only because I put rugs up there first and told him he could."

"You told that dog to lay on my davenport?" Mom asked, eyebrows high on her forehead.

"I figured if he was going to be in the house, I could put rugs out for him because it's a whole lot easier to wash rugs than it is to clean the davenport," Loretta explained.

Dad and I kept quiet. I knew what Dad was thinking, and he knew what I was thinking — if anybody in the whole world could convince my mother to let Needles stay in the house when it was so cold, it would be Loretta.

"And he's been such a good dog," Loretta continued, turning the dust cloth over and over in her hands. "All this time when it's been cold, he's never once tried to sneak in the house, even though you could tell by looking at him that he was miserable. We can't let him suffer."

"He could," Mom said, "stay in the barn. It's warm in the barn."

"He doesn't like staying in the barn," I piped up.

"I don't think he cares to be shut in with the cows," Dad added. "The cows don't take too kindly to him."

"I don't care if he doesn't like the cows," Mom said. "He can stay in the barn."

"But Ma," Dad said, "it's not that he doesn't like the cows—they don't like him. And that makes them nervous. They don't let their milk down so good when they're nervous. You know that."

"Needles makes the cows nervous?" Mom asked.

My father nodded. "He does."

At this point, I did not dare look at Mom or Dad, in case I gave something away. While it was true that some of the cows would chase Needles if given the chance, I had never heard Dad say they were so nervous around the dog that they would not let down their milk.

My father sat on the davenport, and the dog lifted his head and put his chin on Dad's knee. I plopped down on the other side of Needles and began stroking his back. The dog sat up and leaned toward me, licking my cheek. I put my arm around him.

"Just look at them," Loretta said.

My mother blinked. She blinked again. She reached up and pushed her dark hair back off her forehead and heaved a deep sigh. "Oh, all right. Needles can stay in the house—for this afternoon—and I'll think about it."

"But what about toni—"

Dad shot a warning glance in my direction, and I clamped my lips shut.

"Thanks Mom," I said.

"Don't get your hopes up," she muttered. "I might decide he has to stay outside at night, you know."

A little while later, Dad sat down by the kitchen table to put on his work shoes. The sun had set already, and it was time to feed the cows so they could eat their supper while we were eating ours. As Dad threaded the shoestrings through the eyelets of his leather work shoes, Needles hopped off the davenport, trotted into the kitchen and stood by the porch door, tail waving. He glanced at Dad. And then he glanced at the door.

"You know where I'm going, don't you," Dad said, leaning over to scratch Needles' ears.

"Hmmmphhh!" Mom muttered as she set a pan on the stove. "I can't believe it. All afternoon, that dog has been in my house."

I went out to the barn to help Dad feed the cows, and forty-five minutes later, Dad, Needles and I came back to the house.

"Shouldn't we ask Mom first?" I whispered, as Dad held the porch door open so Needles could come inside.

My father shook his head. "Let's just see what happens."

Once we were inside the kitchen, Dad hung up his cap and went to wash his hands. Needles sat down by the porch door, and at any moment, I expected my mother to tell me to put him outside.

Mom turned from the stove.

'Oh, oh,' I thought, 'here it comes…'

"Hold it right there, Needles," Mom said. "Don't take one more step inside this kitchen." She looked at the dog for a moment.

"Are your feet clean?" she asked finally. "Do you have barn lime on your paws?"

I went over to Needles and lifted one front paw. The pad was as clean as it could be.

"His feet are clean," I announced, lifting the other front paw.

"Are you sure?" Mom asked, turning back to the stove so she could stir the green beans with a fork she held in her hand.

Loretta, who had been busy preparing supper, too, came over and lifted one of Needles' paws.

"His feet are clean," she agreed.

"Good," Mom said. "If he's going to stay in the house, his feet have to be clean."

My heart fluttered inside my chest.

"Is Needles going to stay the house?"

"He's in here, isn't he?" Mom replied, sounding grumpy. She dumped the green beans into a colander set in the sink and banged the pan down on the counter.

"Needles," I whispered, "you get to stay in the house." I put my arms around his neck and hugged him.

"Eh? What's that?" Dad asked as he came out of the bathroom.

"Needles gets to stay in the house!" I said.

"But only so long as he behaves himself," Mom said, dumping the green beans back into the pan again. She set the pan on the warm burner.

"Behaves himself?" I asked. "Like how?"

"Like not making messes," Mom replied, adding a pat of butter to the hot green beans. "He's never been house broken, you know."

"He won't make messes, Ma," Dad said, pulling out his chair.

"And how do you know?" Mom asked. She stirred the butter into the green beans.

"Because he won't," Dad said.

"Well, even so, I won't have that dog roaming the house at night." Mom put a cover over the beans and then made her way to the table and sat down. She glanced back and forth, first at me, then at Dad. "I want Needles to be tied in the kitchen at night. We can put his leash around the table leg."

"But—" I stopped abruptly when Dad frowned at me.

"That way, if he messes, it will be on the linoleum, where it's easy to clean up. I won't have him making a smelly mess out of my good carpet."

"Okay, Ma," Dad agreed.

"We can make a special bed for him," Loretta added. She was mashing the potatoes as fiercely as if she were killing a snake. That's what Mom said—that when my sister mashed potatoes she went after them like she was killing a snake. I liked the potatoes when Loretta mashed them. They turned out so fluffy and smooth.

"What kind of a special bed?" I asked.

Needles continued to sit by the door, looking from person to person as we talked.

"Oh," Loretta said, taking down a bowl from the cupboard, "like a nice folded up blanket. That way, he won't get stiff and cold sleeping on the hard floor."

"Hmmmmphhhhh!" Mom snorted. "He's going to sleep in the house where it's warm. That ought to be good enough for him!"

"Now, Ma," Dad said.

"Don't you 'now Ma' me."

"Well—how would you like to sleep on the bare floor at night in the winter?"

"I knew you were going to say that," Mom huffed. "I am not a dog."

"No, you're not," Dad said, "but dogs have feelings, too. Just like people."

"Grrrr-wooof!" Needles commented, ears perked. His jaws snapped open and shut in quick yawn. Then he began panting, and when the tip of his watermelon pink tongue showed between his front teeth, he looked like he was smiling.

"See? Needles says dogs have feelings, too," Dad said.

"Hmmmphhh!" Mom said again.

Loretta piled snowy-white mashed potatoes into a bowl, heaping them in a steaming mound. She put the bowl on the table and turned to Mom. "Should we set a place for Ingman?"

"Well—let's see. He was supposed to be off at three o'clock, and it's what, a little after six now?" Mom said. "I suppose he had to work overtime. Maybe he's working a double shift."

Loretta returned to the sink and began running water into the mashed potato pan. "That's all right, anyway. If Ingman shows up while we're eating, I'll just grab a plate for him," she said, turning off the faucet.

While Mom and Loretta were talking, I noticed Needles had cocked his head to one side.

"Oh," Loretta said as she glanced out the kitchen window, "there he is now. Just coming up the driveway."

A minute later, the kitchen door opened, and Ingman stepped into the house. "Hi, everybody! I'm home! Just in time for supper— wha—?" he said, glancing down at Needles, who was still sitting just inside the door. "Needles! What are you doing in here?"

The dog wriggled over to my big brother, panting and happy to see him. He leaned against Ingman's legs.

"Mom said Needles can stay in the house!" I reported.

"In the house?" Ingman said, leaning down to pet Needles. "Well, and aren't you a lucky dog!"

"You can say that again," Mom said.

Ingman looked over at Mom and flashed her his famous grin, showing his very white and very even teeth. "But it's so cold outside."

Mom sighed. "Oh, I know. I know that now, anyway. I guess I didn't really realize just how cold it was until we went to town this afternoon. I'm not outside much. I mean, I know the thermometer says it's below zero, but, being in the warm house all the time, I guess I forget what that feels like…"

Ingman set down his dinner pail on the counter, hung up his coat, and then came around the table and took his place on the back side. Needles sat down again by the door.

"Needles," Mom said. "Come here."

The dog stood up slowly.

"Needles!" Mom said again. "Come on!"

The dog walked around Loretta's chair to reach my mother, but he didn't look up into her face like he usually did when someone talked to him.

"Now, Needles," Mom said, taking hold of his chin so she could look into his eyes. "No messes in the house. Okay?" Needles stared back at Mom, then he wagged his tail in short, jerky strokes. When Mom released his chin, Needles licked her hand.

"Eeeeuuu," my mother said. "I don't like a dog that licks."

Needles began wagging his tail faster, stepped closer and pushed his nose under Mom's hand.

"All right," Mom said. "That's enough."

Needles stepped back, walked around the table and returned to the porch door. He slid his paws forward, and with a thump, he collapsed on the floor. He rested his nose on one paw, sighed, and closed his eyes.

"The food is getting cold," Mom pointed out. "Let's say our prayer…"

All together, we folded our hands and bowed our heads.

"By thy goodness, all our fed. We thank the Lord for daily bread. Amen."

'And thank you for making it so Needles can stay in the house at night when it's cold,' I added silently.

I looked over at the dog. His rear end wiggled as his tail swept slowly back and forth across the floor. He licked his lips and settled his nose more comfortably on his paw. And as we began to eat supper, Needles fell sound asleep.

"I really can't get over how cold it was outside this afternoon," Mom said, dabbing butter on her mashed potatoes. "Or maybe what I can't get over is that I didn't remember what below zero felt like."

She looked at Needles. Then she looked across the table at Dad.

"You did that on purpose, didn't you," Mom said.

Dad gazed back across the table at her. "Did what on purpose? I told you we could go to town later in the week when it warmed up."

My mother shrugged. "Yes, I guess you did."

Later on when I went out to the barn with Dad, I asked him if it was true that he had wanted to take Mom to the grocery store today "on purpose" when it was below zero.

He reached up to settle his chore cap more firmly on his head.

"What do you think?" he asked.

Enough said.

I should have known Dad would find a way to get my mother outside on the coldest day of the year.

****

~ Acknowledgements ~

Thank you to my husband, Randy Simpson, who, after five books, a how-to book on interviewing people and writing oral histories and a cookbook, still says he's my biggest fan. Randy also is my website designer, my business partner, my administrative assistant, and my book cover designer.

And—like I always say—thank you to my readers, because without readers, writers wouldn't have a job!

****

~ How to Order More Books ~

Here's how to order more copies of *The Coldest Day of the Year*, *Where the Green Grass Grows*, *Cream of the Crop*, *Give Me a Home Where the Dairy Cows Roam*, *Christmas in Dairyland*, *Preserve Your Family History (A Step-by-Step Guide for Interviewing Family Members and Writing Oral Histories)* and *The Rural Route 2 Cookbook:*

• Order on the Internet through Booklocker.com
• Order on the Internet through Amazon.com or Barnes & Noble.
• Order through your local bookstore.
• Call LeAnn at (715) 308-6336.
• Write to LeAnn at E6689 970th Ave.; Colfax, WI 54730
• Order from LeAnn's website—www.ruralroute2.com

When you order books directly from the author (either by calling, writing or ordering through www.ruralroute2.com), you can request autographed copies with personalized inscriptions. Autographed books make great, one-of-a-kind gifts.

****

~ Book Review ~

Give Me a Home Where the Dairy Cows Roam
(Oct. 2004; ISBN-1-59113-592-3; $13.95; www.ruralroute2.com)

Give Me A Home Where The Dairy Cows Roam is a collection of autobiographical stories drawn from author LeAnn Ralph's family dairy farm in Wisconsin in a time when small family farms were commonplace in the Badger State's rural countryside.

Now that we live in a time when approximately 85% of American family dairy farms have disappeared into suburban township developments or absorbed into agribusiness scale corporate farming enclaves, LeAnn takes us back some forty years ago into an era when dairy farming was a dawn-to-dusk life, seven days a week lifestyle that bonded parents and children with hard work and a sense of the land, animals, and homestead that is rapidly passing from today's expanding urban society.

More than just an autobiographical collection of anecdotal stories, *Give Me A Home Where The Dairy Cows Roam* is also enhanced with a recipe for making homemade ice cream without an ice cream maker and a recipe for "Norma's Homemade Bread". Highly recommended reading, *Give Me A Home Where The Dairy Cows Roam* should be on the shelves of every community library in Wisconsin.

James A. Cox, Editor-in-Chief
Midwest Book Review

****

~ Book Review ~

Christmas in Dairyland (True Stories from a Wisconsin Farm)
(August 2003; ISBN 1-59113-366-1; $13.95; www.ruralroute2.com)

Christmas In Dairyland: True Stories From A Wisconsin Farm by
LeAnn R. Ralph is a heartwarming anthology of true anecdotes of
rural life on a Wisconsin dairy farm. Even though Wisconsin is still
known as America's Dairyland, life on a family homestead is fast
being replaced by corporate agribusiness, and the memories treasured
in *Christmas In Dairyland* are quickly becoming unique milestones of
an era needing to be preserved in thought and print for the sake of
future generations. *Christmas In Dairyland* is simply wonderful
reading and is a "must" for all Wisconsin public library collections.

James A. Cox, Editor-in-Chief
Midwest Book Review

****

~ Book Review ~

Cream Of The Crop: More True Stories Form A Wisconsin Farm
(October 2005; ISBN 1591138205; $13.95; www.ruralroute2.com)

Cream of the Crop is the third anthology of biographical and anecdotal stories by LeAnn Ralph about growing up on a Wisconsin dairy farm. In the 1960s there were more than 60,000 dairy farms in Wisconsin, in May of 2004 the Wisconsin Agricultural Statistics Service recorded the number of surviving dairy farms in the state at 15,591. The number has dropped even lower since then. That dairy farming reality is what helps to give LeAnn's deftly told stories their nostalgia for a rural lifestyle that is not-so-slowly disappearing in the Badger state. There are twenty short but immensely entertaining stories in this simply superb anthology. They range from "What's in a Name", to "She'll Be Comin' Round the Cornfield", to "Gertrude and Heathcliff", to the title story "Cream Of The Crop". LeAnn continues to write with a remarkable knack for making people and events come alive in the reader's imagination. Also very highly recommended are LeAnn's two earlier anthologies about life on the family farm in Wisconsin: *Give Me A Home Where The Dairy Cows Roam* (1591135923, $13.95) and *Christmas In Dairyland: True Stories From A Wisconsin Farm* (1591133661, $13.95).

James A. Cox, Editor-in-Chief
Midwest Book Review

****

~ Book Review ~

Preserve Your Family History (A Step-by-Step Guide for
Interviewing Family Members and Writing Oral Histories)
(July 2007; ISBN-13 978-1-60145-239-9;ISBN-10 1-60145-239-X;
$11.95; www.ruralroute2.com)

Preserve Your Family History: A Step-by-Step Guide For
Interviewing Family Members And Writing Oral Histories by LeAnn
R. Ralph is a thoroughly 'user friendly' instruction manual
specifically designed and written for non-specialist general readers
who would like to capture the anecdotal histories of aging family
members whether it would be for supplementing genealogical
research, preserving stories and biographies for the benefit of future
generations, or to simply learn about the life stories of family
members while they are still able to relate them. "Preserve Your
Family History" demonstrates that all that is needed is compiling a
list of people to be interviewed, a set of questions to ask them, a tape
recorder to preserve what is said, a pen and notepad to write on, a
typewriter or computer to put it all down in writing, and above all
else, a willingness to listen. The benefits of recording family
members' oral histories and anecdotal recollections is that their
experiences are the backdrop for your own history, the foundations
for your own value system, opinions, and attitudes, a framework to
explain how you fit into your own family structure. "Preserve Your
Family History" is meant to be a 'consumable,' that is, to be written
in, selected pages photocopied, given to others to utilize in preparing
for interviews, and shared with others in cooperative efforts to
preserve family histories while those who lived and created that
history are still with us. Also very highly recommended for personal
reading, as well as Wisconsin community library collections, are
LeAnn Ralph's "Christmas in Dairyland: True Stories from a
Wisconsin Farm" (2003); "Give Me a Home Where the Dairy Cows
Roam" (2004); "Cream of the Crop: More True Stories from a

Wisconsin Farm" (2005); and "Where The Green Grass Grows: True (Spring and Summer) Stories from a Wisconsin Farm" (2006).

James A. Cox, Editor-in-Chief
Midwest Book Review

****

~ About the Author ~

LeAnn R. Ralph earned an undergraduate degree in English with a writing emphasis from the University of Wisconsin-Whitewater and also earned a Master of Arts in Teaching from UW-Whitewater. She has worked as a newspaper reporter for more than 10 years all together, has taught English at a boys' boarding school, has worked as a substitute teacher and a parish secretary, and is the former editor of the *Wisconsin Regional Writer* (the quarterly publication of the Wisconsin Regional Writers' Assoc.).

The author lives in rural Wisconsin with her husband, one dog, two horses and assorted cats. She is working on her next book, *Candy Cane Summer*, another collection of true stories.

Besides *The Coldest Day of the Year*, LeAnn is the author of the books, *The Rural Route 2 Cookbook* (trade paperback; September 2008; $16.95); *Preserve Your Family History (A Step-by-Step Guide for Interviewing Family Members and Writing Oral Histories)* (e-book; April 2004; trade paperback July 2007; $11.95); *Where the Green Grass Grows* (trade paperback; November 2006; $13.95); *Cream of the Crop* (trade paperback; September 2005; $13.95); *Give Me a Home Where the Dairy Cows Roam* (trade paperback; September 2004; $13.95); *Christmas in Dairyland (True Stories from a Wisconsin Farm)* (trade paperback; August 2003; $13.95).

****

CPSIA information can be obtained at www.ICGtesting.com
Printed in the USA
LVOW072358261212

313357LV00003B/292/P